"You Say **Tomayto...**"

Contrarian Investing in Bitesize Pieces

Alastair Mundy

Hh

HARRIMAN HOUSE LTD
3A Penns Road
Petersfield
Hampshire
GU32 2EW
GREAT BRITAIN

Tel: +44 (0)1730 233870
Email: enquiries@harriman-house.com
Website: www.harriman-house.com

First published in Great Britain in 2012.

978-0857192561

British Library Cataloguing in Publication Data
A CIP catalogue record for this book can be obtained from the British Library.

Printed in the UK by CPI Group (UK) Ltd, Croydon, CR0 4YY.

Disclaimer

Contents

eBook edition

As a buyer of the print edition of *You Say Tomayto* you can now download the eBook edition free of charge to read on an eBook reader, your smartphone or your computer. Simply go to:

http://ebooks.harriman-house.com/yousaytomayto

or point your smartphone at the QRC below.

You can then register and download your eBook copy of the book.

www.harriman-house.com

Acknowledgements

This project would not have been possible without the help of my colleague, Holly Fox. In a moment of insanity Holly offered to make sense of the chaos generated by four years of monthly commentaries. Through a charming combination of suggestion and light requests she persuaded me to rewrite some poorly written parts and clarify others. She also corrected my worst grammatical errors and most embarrassing spelling mistakes. Holly now tells me that, as with 'proper books', I have to accept the blame for any remaining howlers.

Cartoonist Rob Townsend added much with his wonderful cartoons and excruciatingly corny sense of humour. I have almost forgiven him for playing at the wrong tennis club.

It would also be remiss of me to not mention the merry band of contrarian investors I work with: Jo Slater, Peter Lowery, David Lynch, Celia Duncan, Mark Wynne-Jones, Steve Woolley, Leo Liao, Mike du Plessis, and Alessandro Dicorrado. From what I have seen, most contrarian investors are miserable, grumpy, glass half-empty people and it is my privilege to have found nine of them. Investing can at times be a lonely business and working with such loyal, talented, and humble colleagues helps put the fun into fund management. Investing clients' money is a serious business, but it helps not taking yourself too seriously.

The long-suffering and lovely Mrs Mundy (aka Louise) deserves much praise for not just tolerating me for so long, but also encouraging me to turn a random thought into a real plan. She has even stopped moaning about my book mountain. And of course the three little 'doodies', Joel, Max, and Leah, earn credit for making their Dad realise there are far more important things in life than how far the Unilever share price has moved in the last 24 hours.

Many thanks also to my Mum and Dad for their support and love. They appreciated the importance of a decent education, but avoided drumming it into my sister and me. Instead they communicated it in a more subtle way, which has doubtless paid far greater dividends.

A number of friends read various drafts and made some useful suggestions; I found Toni Richards' and Amber Wyatt's feedback particularly helpful. My sister Julia reverted to type and marked her draft with extraordinary diligence and enthusiasm – I now know how it feels to be one of her students. I am also indebted to Suzanne Tull and Myles Hunt at Harriman House, whose expertise transformed my book from a simple draft into a professional publication.

Finally, I am grateful for the support of all my colleagues at Investec Asset Management, who have helped with this project and who are part of the work environment that encourages my investment process. They have allowed me to write about what I believe is relevant, rather than asking that I copy the style of our competitors. I unreservedly apologise to the marketing department for the many rude things I appear to have written about them over the last four years.

About the Author

Alastair Mundy grew up in East London convinced he would play cricket for England. For reasons best known to him, he studied Actuarial Science at City University, London, but after battling his way through the course decided actuarial work was far too boring. Alastair's first job in the real world was a brief stint analysing British government debt (gilts), which drove him to find a position as an equity analyst. He currently works at Investec Asset Management, where he has headed the Contrarian Equity Team for ten years. He is married with three children and remains committed to mastering his second serve.

"It's been bought by a
contrarian investor."

Introduction

It is a particularly self-indulgent act of a fund manager to publish a collection of his monthly commentaries and I am in no position to defend my actions with much substance or fervour. However, feedback received over the years from regular readers suggests that my monthly thoughts are considered more digestible than the standard fare of the investment industry. Investment is not a dry subject and I believe the technical jargon commonly found in some industry publications is employed primarily to persuade the reader of the author's intellectual superiority.

Commentary writing can be a blight on fund managers' lives, somewhere between monthly compliance meetings and completing training logs. Our marketing departments constantly urge us to review the prior month and then offer a forecast for the coming ones. Rather than conform resentfully, I write on topics I find interesting, stimulating, or even puzzling. I dare say when my marketing department notices I have strayed, I will be hung upside down by my toenails and instructed to correct my ways.

This collection of notes should not be read as a 'How To' guide of contrarian investing; it is instead intended as a base from which to explore the complex, broad, and fascinating subjects of investment analysis and fund management. Most of the areas considered have been researched in much greater depth by experts. Often I have simply raised one or two of their most relevant or revealing thoughts. I hope to encourage fellow investors to think less about why GlaxoSmithKline rose by 0.5% last month, and more about the factors most likely to determine its price in five years' time.

The merits of contrarian investing are documented in a number of ways over the following pages. Although I'm sure my wife considers my bloody-mindedness and stubbornness as being perfect qualifications for a contrarian investor, the approach is a little different than she assumes. Yes, it requires one to act against the crowd. However, it is futile to do so without good reason. A naïve contrarian investor pops into a pub looking for a fight and is delighted if his first opponent is Lennox Lewis. A more seasoned contrarian looks to fight only little old ladies and small children. But, looking for the right opponent in my local pub in Upminster is far from straightforward – little old ladies can sometimes be veteran jujitsu champions – and detecting the easier battles in the stock market is similarly challenging. At first blush, many stocks are optically attractive and other appealing stocks may initially look like dogs.

There is no trustworthy shortcut (that we have found anyway) to separate the dogs from the delightful. The long cut is the implementation of much hard work. Not hard work as in coalmining or ten hour days on a building site, but hard work as in understanding a company's business model, why other investors hate it, what positive factors they might have missed, how its balance sheet and cash flow interact, and whether its valuation is sufficiently attractive. None of that is rocket science (although my colleagues who actually conduct the analysis may disagree), but that does not make it easy. The bull arguments are often well hidden and can only be discovered through meticulous work, a sceptical mindset, and deep thought.

Contrarian investing offers fruitful rewards to an investor, but can sometimes prove a tortuous approach. The technology bubble of the late 1990s was little fun and the mining bubble a few years ago did nothing for my blood pressure. At such times, the crowd, convinced that recent events have changed the world forever, rationalises new investment paradigms. Perfectly good stocks are sold to fund the new, new thing. However, it is during these tough periods that, providing they don't lose their jobs, the real contrarians can distinguish themselves from their impostors and load up with great ideas for the next investment cycle. Eventually, the market realises the new paradigm is the emperor with no clothes and normal service is resumed.

Alastair Mundy

1.

You Say Tomayto

Beneath the Skin of Contrarian Investing

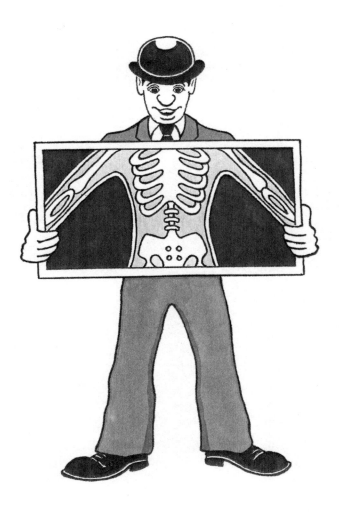

You say tomayto

I was once encouraged by a colleague to be less open when discussing our contrarian investment process. He was concerned that I would let the cat out of the bag and successfully convert a plethora of non-believers to our ways. I couldn't blame his motivation for the suggested vow of silence; he clearly recognised that we were one-trick ponies and worried that if our behaviour was copied by other investors, any competitive advantage would soon be arbitraged away, requiring us to put a hoof in the air and admit defeat.

Whilst undoubtedly over-rating my evangelical skills, I thought he also missed some vital points that suggested contrarian investing would remain a minority sport. It is not easy implementing a contrarian

> "It is not easy implementing a contrarian strategy"

strategy. Many investors are uncomfortable acting against the crowd and even if they 'know' it is the correct course of action, will still strive to avoid it. Eminent economist John Maynard Keynes was spot on when he commented that "worldly wisdom teaches that it is better for reputation to fail conventionally than to succeed unconventionally".

However, as important is the consideration that, because none of us can accurately forecast the future, our competitors might be correct in opposing our investment opinions. We model ourselves as historians, rather than all-knowing astrologers, spending a significant amount of time piecing together the past and trying to ascertain whether published accounts are accurate records of what occurred. We make no promises about the future. It is purely guesswork – albeit educated guesswork.

This guesswork determines that we assess a series of facts and make a judgement on how they will shape the future. But our conclusions are just one view. For example, we may feel a company's executive remuneration scheme over-rewards the recipients for good results while avoiding penalties for failure. However, other investors may believe that the structure ensures management and shareholders are perfectly aligned and incentivises management successfully. Likewise, some may regard a company that keeps its capital expenditure similar to its depreciation as an efficient capital allocator, but others may believe it is under-investing in the business. Investors might believe a poorly managed company can be shaken up or be on the slippery slope to bankruptcy or that a company generating a high return on capital exhibits high barriers to entry or excessive and unsustainable returns. There is a yin to every yang, a Morecambe to every Wise, and a 'tomayto' to every 'tomahto'.[1]

In its simplest form, one could argue that this difference of views is a 50/50 bet; no different to tossing a coin. However, the wager we make is more complex because in stock market analysis there are a number of outcomes with different probabilities of occurrence and a variety of pay-offs. We search for those stocks with an attractive pay-off if the outcome is as we expect, but that will inflict a relatively small loss if we are wrong.

Of course, the most important reason why my evangelising should be of limited concern is that more erudite and articulate investors and academics than me have tried and failed. There have been numerous books and academic studies published on the merits of contrarian and value investing, but despite this, the majority still wish to practise alternative investment religions.

I think it is safe to ignore my colleague's pleas. We are left with the bizarre ambition that we wish to persuade our clients that our contrarian principles have some merit, whilst simultaneously hoping that our competitors remain convinced that we are clueless.

December 2011

---

[1]Although the nature of our investment style dictates that we sometimes feel lonely, the presence of investors with opposing views suits us well as it provides the liquidity after which we hanker. These investors sell to us when we are buying and buy from us when we are selling. (Annoyingly, our analysis suggests that both sets of investors make good money from us, at least in the short term.) It is a much greater challenge to invest and disinvest when running with the herd.

Too scared to watch?

I was recently asked to prepare a presentation that contained a case study of a stock within the portfolio. Obviously, I was tempted to showcase a brilliant investment that illustrated foresight, a clear and perceptive mind and a fantastic talent in timing, but frankly I couldn't see the point. Every investor should, after all, be able to dig up a couple of examples of some good stock picks. At best, they probably reflect a decent mixture of luck and skill, but with clever use of hindsight a presenter can persuade an audience that skill was the major contributor.

This exercise of reliving past glories in front of an audience is particularly futile for an investor in out-of-favour stocks. It is rather like, as a kid, watching an episode of *Doctor Who*[2] for a second time. You know the plot, you know that really nasty things never happen to the Doctor, and therefore you don't need to hide behind the sofa. But remember how scared you were the first time? Our vital job when presenting, is to recreate the conditions at the time of purchase, not at the time of sale, and typically we find it difficult to explain or even remember quite how uncomfortable we felt. Without those emotions the story lacks meaning.

Any investment argument we make can be separated into two lists: one with the positive motives for buying a stock and the second with some good motives for passing. A falling share price supports those investors who energetically espouse the negatives. Although at these moments we do our best to remain calm and deal with facts alone, the decision never involves just black or white; usually we are

---

[2] Long-running British TV science-fiction series featuring the eponymous Time Lord. Doctor Who explores the universe in his time machine-spacecraft, thwarting the evil plans of countless extra-terrestrials. His arch-adversaries, the cyborg Daleks, plot world domination and the extermination of all non-Dalek life. Being virtually impenetrable to most weapons and equipped with a death ray that can kill anything, the Daleks have the innate ability to scare small children witless; this is despite having what appears to be a sink plunger welded to their heads (see cartoon).

"You can come out now, kids ...
Doctor Who's finished."

offered slightly different shades of grey and it is tough to act rationally. We are only human and our confidence may be knocked after buying the shares at a higher level or having heard a particularly strong counter-argument.

To simulate the feelings when buying a deeply unloved stock, I generally encourage an audience to imagine eating alone in a restaurant.

"It is tough to act rationally"

For most of us it is a deeply unpleasant experience. We can start by reading the menu and wine list and checking our mobiles, but when these distractions have passed it is hard to relax. All around us happy groups of people are wining, dining, talking, and laughing. Every now and again, we catch someone's eye and they give us a look of what can only be read as pity. After all, no one would choose to eat alone. We assume they see us as sad, lonely, and friendless. This experience is repeated a number of times as we scan the restaurant and, when the food finally arrives, our heart is pumping and we will eat a lot faster than other diners, before inevitably leaving our table first and with great relief. (Standing up at a football match in the home end and applauding the referee for giving a 50/50 decision to the away team will probably elicit similar feelings, but is probably more dangerous than is necessary to appreciate the merits of contrarian investing.)

Of course, just experiencing these feelings associated with acting alone doesn't guarantee success. Often the consensus is correct (Brazil being favourites to win the World Cup doesn't guarantee their failure), or sometimes the risks are simply not worth taking because the rewards aren't sufficiently attractive. We regard the nausea, increased blood pressure and general sense of unease as being necessary, but definitely not sufficient conditions to make many of our investments. To the mix must also be added hard work and diligent analysis.

May 2010

Portfolio concentration – separating the good from the great

Clients and potential clients often request a breakdown of our performance by individual stock, i.e. an attribution analysis. It would, obviously, be great to provide a list containing only successful stock picks. However, performance is not like that. Historically, we have found that even those stocks we have purchased that have performed well over longer periods have had variable short-term returns. Add to this list our losers and it is clear that we will always generate a mixture of positive and negative returns. In fact, over the long term, virtually all investors can point to a spread of a few very good ideas, a greater number of decent picks, a fair number of poor ones, and one or two howlers.

> "If you can tell a good investment from a bad one, you can also distinguish a great one from a good one"

If this is the case, shouldn't we just invest in our really great ideas and avoid the rest? I have changed my beliefs on this over the years. I previously thought that at purchase it was too hard to distinguish the best ideas from the rest and that significant diversification was a necessity. However, I have now converted to successful value investor Seth Klarman's view: "If you can tell a good investment from a bad one, you can also distinguish a great one from a good one". The stumbling block to implementing a great ideas strategy, however, is that we simply cannot always find sufficient stars to fill a portfolio to allow our clients to sleep comfortably at night.

For example, when we purchased our last pieces of Travis Perkins and Signet Jewelers (after several attempts at higher prices) we were reasonably confident, on a probability-weighted basis, that we were buying some very cheap shares. At the time, however, the market in general, and these stocks in particular, were distressed. Opportunities like this occur rarely. If we held only stocks where we could match that level of confidence, our portfolio would be either highly liquid or one with few stocks. Portfolios with those characteristics would rarely be permitted under most clients' mandates and, even if possible, would typically display such high volatility that few investors would have the stomach for the journey. While Klarman warns that it is vital not to confuse volatility with risk, I would imagine most clients are not so forgiving.

Some fund managers are comfortable with this strategy. Warren Buffett has always run a fairly tight portfolio and his business partner Charlie Munger at times has had what most would consider an absurdly tight portfolio. However, even Munger cannot escape from the problem of skewed attribution: "If you took our top fifteen decisions out, we'd have a pretty average record".[3]

Interestingly, a reasonable amount of academic research supports the strategy of investing only in one's best ideas. For example, Cohen, Polk, and Silli[4] found:

> The stock that active managers display the most conviction towards ex-ante, outperforms the market, as well as the other stocks in those managers' portfolios, by approximately one to four percent per quarter depending on the benchmark employed ... The other stocks managers hold do not exhibit significant outperformance. This leads

---

[3] Munger, Charles T., *Poor Charlie's Almanack: The Wit and Wisdom of Charles T. Munger* (Donning Company Publishers, 2005).

[4] Cohen, Randolph B., Christopher K. Polk, and Bernhard Silli, *Best Ideas* (Social Science Research Network, 2009).

us to two conclusions. First, the US stock market does not appear to be efficiently priced … Second, the organization of the money management industry appears to make it optimal for managers to introduce stocks into their portfolio that are not outperformers. We argue that investors would benefit if managers held more concentrated portfolios.

Given our remit of managing a fund that must always be at least 80% invested in UK equities, how can we best use these findings? To reduce the risk of buying underperformers, we believe it is vital to hold cash when we have insufficient ideas to maintain a fully invested portfolio, and to reduce volatility, we are content to build some 'index-aware' positions. The world's great investors may sneer at this strategy and others may accuse us of index hugging, but we believe it is very important to reduce volatility to a level with which our clients are comfortable.

February 2010

The risks of structural decline – a requiem to fondue sets

Catching falling knives was a reasonably fruitless activity in 2011. In fact, several of the worst market performers in 2010 were poor once again last year. As contrarian investors, we must question whether anything has changed to adversely affect our style of investing in out-of-favour shares. Is contrarian investing heading the same way as boy bands, Curly Wurlys,[5] fondue sets, and shaggy perms?

In our view, some rules of engagement have changed significantly. The first is the influence of the economic and financial backdrop. Company turnarounds are most straightforward when economic conditions are sound; there is simply more turnover within an industry to share between the various protagonists. In weaker times, the battle for turnover is intense and the weaker players struggle to recover their poise. As turnarounds require the support and patience of banks, they are even tougher if financing opportunities are scarce. To take one example, Dixons Retail has refurbished its UK stores (Currys and PC World) and re-trained its historically unenthusiastic staff, but the debt burden it carries has hampered this process. Despite most independent commentators reacting positively to the changes at Dixons Retail, its market share has continued to fall as competitor intensity (from Amazon, John Lewis, and superstores) has increased in a declining market.

The second noteworthy change is technological. It is interesting that even forecasts of technological progress made by the most fervent analysts in the late 1990s technology boom were

---

[5] A Cadbury creation dating from the 1970s – a tasty but oddly-shaped chocolate-caramel lattice. The bars were once very popular, but now account for less than 0.1% of the company's sales in Britain.

"Is contrarian investing heading the same way as boy bands, Curly Wurlys, fondue sets, and shaggy perms?"

insufficiently bullish. Technology has subsequently developed extraordinarily quickly and, in the process, has destroyed a number of business models that had endured for decades. For example, regional newspapers (an area where as investors we continue to embarrass ourselves) appear to have lost their monopolies in recruitment and classified advertising to online competitors. Now that we can surf the net to find houses for sale and pubs that need chefs, it is unlikely that former glories such as these will be revived.

Each generation probably believes that the changes it experiences are more meaningful and wider-reaching than others. But the effect that technological progress has had on companies in retailing, media (and even technology) industries in particular, suggests this claim currently has some credibility.

So how should a contrarian investor respond if conditions are less propitious? We have always warned against catching *all* falling knives and stress the importance of detailed balance sheet analysis of every potential investment. Without long-term financing, a weakly capitalised company must recover quickly. We prefer to, where possible, minimise our balance sheet concerns so that the companies we own have sufficient time to manufacture a turnaround.

In addition to a sound balance sheet – and importantly we demand it is sound across a number of future scenarios – there are other indicators that we believe help to improve our hit rate when we purchase out-of-favour stocks.

The quantum of companies' operational underperformance can vary across industries. In some industries, particularly those in which companies have established brands, market shares are reasonably stable and declines can be relatively slow. However, in others, particularly those more fashion related or commoditised, market shares are more volatile – and once lost are much harder to regain.[6]

This volatility of market share often arises in industries that have few barriers to entry, thus allowing 'brands' to grow very quickly. It is, for example, interesting to see how quickly aggregators (such as Confused.com and CompareTheMarket.com) have rapidly built brands and won large market shares in the motor insurance market. Similarly, supermarkets have built substantial market shares in many non-food related products over the last decade. To make matters worse, they have been comfortable selling products as loss leaders, thus dragging down overall industry profitability as price competition bites.

It is also revealing to consider barriers to exit. If it is too expensive for a company to leave an industry (because of, for example, onerous lease payments), it may be forced to remain in the market and thus reduce the returns for other profitable competitors.

Few of these considerations are clear-cut. Industry dynamics can change, even following stability over several decades, and share prices can move quickly to discount a new era. As a rule of thumb, we now prefer to search for underperforming companies in industries where market shares move slowly and reasonable barriers to entry exist, and we are ever more diligent in our balance sheet analysis.

January 2012

---

[6] As an incurable romantic, I was appalled last season to see my son and his mates use cricket bats made by Adidas and Nike (heavens above, is nothing sacred?). These manufacturers have muscled their way into a market previously monopolised by the nostalgia-inducing names of, amongst others, Duncan Fearnley, Gray Nicholls, and Stuart Surridge.

"We've got another one who's
tried catching falling knives!"

Mean reversion – whatever goes up probably comes down

There has been much talk of bond bubbles recently and some commentators have tied their colours firmly to the mast. Nassim Taleb, the author of *Fooled by Randomness*, was quoted in the *Financial Times* recommending that every single human being ought to bet against US Treasuries as it was a 'no brainer'.[7]

It is interesting that there is far less chatter highlighting the bubble-like characteristics of profit margins (profits as a percentage of sales). After all, many companies in the US and Europe are currently generating high margins. Historically, this has proved a mean-reverting series (for the non-mathematicians, 'whatever goes up goes back down'), although strangely enough, it is quite hard to find many strategists discussing this possibility. Instead, individual companies are typically lauded for generating higher margins as, to many, it indicates organisations in rude health.

Margins are high for a number of reasons. Low interest rates and tax rates have contributed and cost-cutting, be it on labour or more general costs, has clearly had a major influence. In the short term it is likely costs will be tightly controlled, especially as management are generally highly incentivised to reach their targets. There may be individual hiccups along the way (is there a correlation between penny-pinching on health and safety and the incidence of oil spills?), but the rule of thumb seems to be: keep cutting until the pips squeak – and then cut some more.

Another contributor to margin accretion, although not always highlighted by official statistics, must be price inflation. There is no doubt that my Marks & Spencer's socks and pants are not as long-lasting as they were twenty years ago (and I have no reason to believe

---

[7] Davis, Jonathan, 'Beware the ending of a bond epic', *Financial Times*, 5 September, 2010.

"**Individual companies are typically lauded for generating higher margins as, to many, it indicates organisations in rude health**"

I wear them harder). Has a reduction in prices accompanied a reduction in quality? Well, they are lower priced, but I'm not convinced they are low enough to justify the reduction in quality. While the plural of anecdote is not data, it is not just clothes providing a lower quality to price ratio. Furniture, toys, and a variety of household goods all seem to have significantly shorter life expectancies. It would be fascinating to see some research in this area.

Both cost-cutting and subtle price inflation can continue for some time. Of course, a company's cost-cutting eats into other companies' revenues and consumers' jobs, while price inflation erodes all consumers' disposable incomes. This may be a story of gradual movements rather than step changes, but we are certainly not betting on a new paradigm of structurally higher margins.

August 2010

Tesco – every little helps margins revert

One issue that has concerned us for some time is the high level of operating margins generated by a number of listed companies in the UK stock market. Indeed, several companies are producing their highest ever margins and most are much closer to their peak than their trough. Our belief in mean reversion drives our scepticism that companies can continue to achieve such high levels of returns. Clients questioning this belief typically challenge us to explore the reasons for margin erosion. One possible reason is increased competition and Tesco's woes provide an interesting case study in this regard.

Tesco's profit warning on 12 January 2012 was a surprise to the market (as evidenced by the 16% fall in share price on the day). Tesco's top brass had encouraged investors to regard the company as a master of its destiny – a company sufficiently large to set the rules in the UK food retailing sector and manage its domestic business to produce an operating margin consistently around 6%.

Tesco's market-leading margin had been generated historically by passing on its huge buying power over suppliers on to customers in lower prices, consequently encouraging growth in shoppers and therefore turnover. In its glory days, Tesco's virtuous circle of lower prices and high volumes discouraged competitive reaction from smaller competitors.

The theory – and for a time, the practice – was fine, but something evidently went wrong. Perhaps Tesco started to milk UK profitability to feed its international ambitions or maybe management's over-confidence handed other food retailers the opportunity to catch up. Whatever the reason, and despite the huge amount of capital expenditure that Tesco has recently committed to the UK, Morrisons, Sainsbury's, and Asda have eroded its market share.

In a desperate attempt to maintain its margins Tesco started pulling other levers. For example, according to Oriel Securities, over the last five years the amount of square foot per member of staff in the UK has risen by 24%. (This is not a perfect statistic to use given the confusion created by the high growth in recent years of labour-intensive Tesco Expresses and labour-light non-food space, but there is little doubt that the trend is correct.) Whilst a short-term positive for profitability, this has affected service levels and resulted in longer checkout queues and emptier shelves. Also, Tesco's reputation for low prices has been damaged and customer perceptions in some surveys suggest that Tesco is now considered the least competitive of the big four. Interestingly enough, on price check surveys Tesco is more competitive than its customers believe. It might be that Tesco ensures the prices of the least surveyed goods are the most uncompetitive, or it may simply suggest that it is finding it difficult to convince its customers that its prices really are competitive. Either way the company has a problem.

Under its new chief executive Philip Clarke, Tesco immediately responded with a significant increase in staffing and other costs. It is unclear what the longer-term impact of Tesco's profits warning will be on the food retailing sector, but the immediate impact is a reduction in margins of the market leader. A company generating supernormal margins has been reined in by a combination of its customers and its competition. Tesco (which we are currently analysing in detail – we will share our conclusions at a later date) may be the 'canary in the coalmine'[8] or simply a one-off. The stock market is betting on the latter and remains sanguine about the strength of corporate profitability. If this assumption is incorrect, the lower equity market volatility of the last few months may well prove short-lived.

April 2012

---

[8] It used to be common practice that coal miners carried caged canaries with them; if poisonous gases were present in the tunnels, the canary would show symptoms before the miner, acting as an early-warning system.

Risk management – dinner party do's and don'ts

The asset management industry has grown substantially over the last twenty years, and some pockets have expanded phenomenally. Areas such as compliance, hedge funds, and marketing have grown faster than any sane forecaster would have predicted. The benefits each of these has brought to clients are questionable, but for another day. However, the growth of risk management from cottage industry to behemoth is worthy of discussion.

Perhaps this is the most straightforward growth story. After all, who wouldn't wish to assess risk more carefully if provided with the opportunity? Once clever software packages allowed asset managers, and just as importantly their clients, to assess if risk was under control, it was impossible to put the cat back in the bag. 'Shall we do less risk analysis' is an unlikely vote-winner for a pension fund trustee or city professional whose greatest fear is probably an outsized legal claim against them for negligence.

This would be well and good if this thorough analysis of portfolios, their vulnerabilities and sensitivities was actually beneficial. Sadly, it is not. I will not defend that statement with any deep intellectual insight, but merely point out that an extraordinary global financial crisis struck when risk analysis budgets were at all-time highs. (The absurd counter-argument from risk experts is that we should imagine how much worse it could have been if their superb modelling hadn't been used.)

The main snag with all the risk packages is that they assume previous combinations of circumstances will repeat. So, if a company's share price has always jiggled around a lot, it always will, or if stock A and stock B have always moved together then, likewise, they always will. While I am aware of the importance of history, this does smack of constantly fighting the last war.

Although I have little respect for the modern methods of measuring risk, I wholeheartedly accept the need for risk management. My preference is to approach it with a greater degree of common sense. Over the years, I have often compared portfolio management to hosting a dinner party.[9] No seasoned host would invite just the six or eight funniest friends they have: convention dictates their friends' less amusing partners must be invited too – probably a good thing as funny people are not always the best listeners. And even funny people ultimately run out of jokes, leaving a vacuum to be filled with a random football trivia question or philosophical puzzle. And when that doesn't work, there is always a place for 'Where are you going on holiday this year?' (Mrs Mundy's party piece). The most successful parties and series of parties therefore need a good mix of invitees. And portfolios are no different: a number of stocks bought at a variety of times for a host of reasons can bring great strength to a portfolio.

Admittedly, that does read like the *Janet and John*[10] guide to portfolio risk management, but it is not always necessary to make a simple subject complex (unless you are a consultant charging ridiculous fees). Of course, the analogy can be taken further. There are some 'friends' who you should never invite to a dinner party and there are also some stocks or assets that should never be in a portfolio. Inevitably the absolute turn-off is excessive valuation.

Some clients might use performance as a shortcut to assess portfolio risk. After all, a fund manager who consistently outperforms his peers must, in their eyes, be doing something right.

---

[9] Coming from Essex I have never even been invited to a dinner party, let alone hosted one, so please indulge me here.

[10] A series of learn-to-read books used in UK primary schools from the 1950s to 1970s featuring two siblings from an unashamedly middle-class family.

Unfortunately, the best fund managers over medium-term periods have sometimes proved particularly dangerous custodians of clients' money. It is almost as though these managers

"A number of stocks bought at a variety of times for a host of reasons can bring great strength to a portfolio"

have convinced themselves they can control absolutely anyone at their parties and have therefore taken to creating increasingly bizarre guest lists. Eventually, the party goes horribly wrong.

February 2012

Stretching the analogy

Some common feedback we currently receive is that many potential stock market participants would prefer to wait until 'things are less uncertain' before committing extra funds to equity markets. In an ideal world, this is a perfect strategy. However, stock markets rarely behave in an ideal way. 'Less uncertainty' usually equates to a mixture of better economic news, better corporate results, confidence that the worst of the large negative surprises are behind us, and a greater flow of cash into equities. Unfortunately, when these factors can finally be ticked off a checklist, we will probably be closer to the top of the market than the bottom.

So, rather than waiting for less uncertainty, the equity investor looking to maximise his returns would probably benefit more if he dealt only in periods of **great** uncertainty. Conditions might become even more uncertain (i.e. worse) and prices fall further, but providing he was buying well below fair value it would not be a long-term problem.

Our stock purchases are analogous to pulling an elastic band. It is never clear how far the elastic band will stretch, but ultimately it will do one of two things: bounce back, or break. Imagine the elastic band can be pulled back a total of x notches, but that no-one knows what x is. Someone playing this game will be rewarded the longer he waits for it to bounce back, **provided** he does finally bet on it bouncing back. The only way he doesn't win is if the elastic band breaks. On the other hand, he definitely **cannot** win if he never bets on the elastic band bouncing back. And obviously he will win far less (and possibly even lose), if he waits for the elastic band to bounce back before placing his bet.

Taking the game a bit further, it makes no sense for the player to make bets on when the elastic band bounces back if he knows that

> "Stock markets rarely behave in an ideal way"

a large number of bands actually break and that the money he makes on those bouncing back will not cancel out the losers. While this tortuous analogy has been 'stretched' to its limit, it is very useful in explaining our strategy so far in 2008.

i.   We know we have to deal in uncertain times. Whenever all participants are certain and bullish, markets are typically expensive and ready to fall.

ii.   We have a number of elastic bands (stocks) in case some do break (fall significantly).

iii. We are happy to buy stocks provided they have already stretched significantly from their fair value.

iv.   If they stretch even further we are happy buying more, providing that we still believe they will bounce back.

v.   We won't keep betting more and more on a bounce-back. We will sometimes simply maintain our position.

vi.   If we lose confidence in the bounce-back, or worry that a break has become more likely, or can find other stocks where we believe the odds of a bounce-back/break are more attractive, we are happy switching.

vii. The stocks most attractive to us are those that offer significant gains from a bounce-back combined with the lowest probability of a break.

August 2008

Navel gazing

At the end of every calendar year most investors seem happy to share their hopes and fears for the year ahead. Several of them are also content to provide forecasts for market levels. We have always emphasised that there is little science and even less accuracy in this process. Commonly, these forecasts are accompanied with specific timings ('tough first half, but better second half') as if the primary question is simply not exacting enough. We do not participate in such competitions as firstly, we know we would likely be wrong and, secondly, we don't really understand the market's obsession with calendar year returns.

The time saved avoiding this exercise has allowed us to conduct some 'navel gazing' on our investment process. Two areas we have been considering are patience and low portfolio activity; many of the best investors over a number of decades share these characteristics.

Patience is a fascinating subject. As contrarian investors, we are often guilty of buying and selling too early. While neither of these are sins in themselves – after all when asked how he had become so rich, Baron Jacob Rothschild commented, "I made my fortune while selling always a little too early" – we think we could improve our process by not always buying so early. The institutional imperative that demands continual outperformance probably increases one's desire to deal, as does the extraordinary amount of (useless) information to which everyone has access. The ability to wait patiently for only the best ideas is not easily gained, but pays great rewards. Baron Philippe de Rothschild (clearly from a family that both invested well and were eminently quotable) once exclaimed that the time to buy was "when there is blood in the streets".

Some clients wonder if our emphasis on patience and low turnover (on average we hold our stocks for three years, compared to an industry average of between six and nine months) is justified

"The ability to wait patiently for only the best ideas is not easily gained, but pays great rewards"

given the speed at which markets move in the modern era. While this is a relevant question, this 'speed' should not be confused with 'distance'. For example, equity markets have taken nine years ('distance') to de-rate to their current levels from their valuation peak, despite some intermittent bouts of extreme volatility ('speed'). This is true for stocks too: think about the steady decline and de-rating of formerly successful companies such as ITV and Rentokil – more a grind than a collapse.

The successful application of patience is difficult (thankfully, otherwise we would be unemployed), but we continue trying to learn from our and others' mistakes. Sitting on our hands waiting for the right time to act and then avoiding selling too early are just some of our New Year's resolutions.

December 2008

Contrarian investing – cycling through the haze

When shares are falling, many investors wait for a catalyst or at least some 'increased visibility' before buying. This virtually ensures they will miss the bottom. If they are reluctant to change their sometimes entrenched views, they may also miss a significant amount of the initial burst of performance from the lows. We believe it is essential to capture this early part of the performance cycle, and with no-one waving a flag at the bottom, an investor must purchase early. This demands that investors must buy into a story that by definition is considered increasingly unattractive.

Not surprisingly, the investor acting in this way is deemed to have lost the plot. John Maynard Keynes summed it up elegantly:

> "For it is the essence of his behaviour that he should be eccentric, unconventional and rash in the eyes of average opinion. If he is successful, that will only confirm the general belief in his rashness; and if in the short run he is unsuccessful, which is very likely, he will not receive much mercy."

In preference to fine-tuning both our share purchases and profit expectations for a company, we instead assess the average level of profits the company can achieve over the medium term. To borrow from Keynes once again, it is more important for this forecast to be

"Investors must buy into a story that by definition is considered increasingly unattractive"

"approximately right rather than precisely wrong". An average stock market rating typically accompanies the attainment of an average level of profits, so if we can buy the company's shares at a meaningful discount to the product of these numbers then sizeable profits can be generated.

Of course, this won't always work. The company's future average level of profitability may be much lower than history suggests, or a company's existing capital structure may restrict the expected level of profits. However, providing this approach works on average, the relevance of each individual stock attaining its expected level of profitability is reduced. When we perform this exercise we are certainly not refuting the likelihood of a downturn or denying the possibility that a downturn may be quite deep; we are simply taking a longer-term view instead.

March 2008

2.

Circles of Competence

Expertise, Luck, or Sheer Bloody-Mindedness?

Circles of competence – Tony the Cabbie

I have a friend, Tony, a minicab driver, whom I first met as a client when he was driving for the local minicab firm. On that first job, after transporting me safely to my destination he entrepreneurially suggested that it would be financially beneficial to both of us if, in future, we cut out the middleman and I used him directly.

Over the years I have shared many journeys and conversations with Tony. Sharing a conversation is an overstatement, as our dialogues are about 80/20 weighted in his favour. However, he assures me this is best for both of us, because the biggest risk for a passenger is the driver falling asleep at the wheel; something he is much less likely to do if he is talking. I have therefore listened to Tony a lot and we have covered numerous subjects. These have ranged from football – speciality: Dagenham and Redbridge FC – to chess, asylum seekers, religion, and cars. (We've even discussed the potential for a TV-like wife swap, but that was admittedly on one of our longer journeys.) In fact, I struggle to think of any subject, other than ballet, where Tony did not have a great deal to share with me.

Tony is a good mate and undoubtedly a bright guy. Providing his passenger knows nothing about the areas on which he is being educated, he would assume Tony is an expert on several subjects. Actually, Tony is pretty sure that he is an expert on several subjects. Despite my protests that he can't be that clever and worldly wise, he remains convinced that he is a purveyor of only the very highest material.[11]

I wouldn't be surprised if there are loads of 'Tonys' out there driving cabs. However, I fear there are many in other professions

---

[11] His mum agrees, see 'The Audience Fights Back – From: Tony's Mum' (page 182).

"A tendency to believe we have far greater knowledge than we actually possess is widespread"

too, not least fund management. In general, a tendency to believe we have far greater knowledge than we actually possess is widespread. In a cab driver this weakness is irrelevant, but in a fund manager it can be fatal.

This is why Warren Buffett has so often spoken about understanding one's 'circle of competence'[12]:

> Intelligent investing is not complex, though that is far from saying that it is easy. What an investor needs is the ability to correctly evaluate selected businesses. Note that word 'selected': You don't have to be an expert on every company, or even many. You only have to be able to evaluate companies within your circle of competence. The size of that circle is not very important; knowing its boundaries, however, is vital.

If we look at Buffett's larger investments, his circles of competence are apparently the results of his formative years: soft drinks, investment banks, trains, sweets, and newspapers.[13] Over time, Buffett has expanded his circle of competence by a limited amount, and typically only when encouraged by his sidekick Charlie Munger. Munger is keen to discover new circles of competence – "strive to become a little wiser every day" – but he also stresses the risks of stretching too far:

> You have to figure out where your own abilities are. If you play games where other people have the ability and you do not, you are going to lose. That is as close to certain as any prediction that I can make. You have to figure out where you have an edge. And you have got to play within your own circle of competence.

---

[12] Buffett, Warren, 1996 Shareholders' Letter, 28 February 1997.

[13] See 'Fancy a Crunchie? Not at that price' (page 55), for my forays into sweet research.

It is one step appreciating the need for a circle of competence; it is a larger step identifying it. If part of our job is to confidently answer all clients' queries it is difficult admitting to our limits and weaknesses.

Actually, I think the major problem is appreciating when we know enough to **have** a circle of competence. We can never know, or even want to know, everything about an industry, but it is useful to have a rough idea about what we don't understand: we need to assess how damaging that lack of knowledge could be. For example, we all learned a great deal about investment banking as the Global Financial Crisis developed and this should have knocked the confidence of all but the most confident of bank investors. The highly geared nature of banks and the large (negative) numbers that were bandied about from the start of the crisis might well have triggered sufficient warning lights for many.

Alternatively, an investor in a well-financed asset-backed food retailer may believe there is far less information that he doesn't know and that it is unlikely to be information that will significantly affect the future of the company. Obviously this higher level of confidence does not on its own justify the purchase of the company's shares, but it may encourage the investor to wait patiently for an attractively priced buying opportunity.

As we age, humility increasingly impacts our thinking and we have a growing appreciation of the limits of our knowledge. This tends to reduce our circles of competence, but I am far from convinced this is detrimental to long-term performance. In fact, perhaps fund management is a skill that improves with age. Let's hope so.

March 2011

Expertise – keep practising

I have just passed the 26th anniversary of my Further Maths mock A-level, and although time has proven a great healer, I am pretty sure I scored a rather unremarkable 23%. This proved an excellent lead indicator for the real event and come the following August I was awarded an O grade, a mark that suggested I had learned nothing in the two years subsequent to my maths O-level.

My parents were, it is fair to say, unimpressed with this result. However, as a glass half full man, I did muster some positives. It was fairly obvious that there were some extremely intelligent people I was competing against, and any thoughts I might have had of building a career based on academic superiority were evidently a non-starter. That was a better lesson to learn at 18 than 38.

Assuming I didn't benefit from a late intellectual growth spurt (a fair assumption based on the actions of those who marked my degree papers) I marched into an industry where conventional wisdom would claim I was at a distinct disadvantage. I say this as I often hear references to individuals who are 'really smart' or 'extraordinarily bright' in a way that implies this quality gives them an inherent advantage over us mere mortals.

But is this conventional wisdom correct? Well, Warren Buffett certainly does not regard a lack of super-intelligence as a hindrance. In fact, he considers it an impediment: "If you have a 150 IQ, sell 30 points to someone else. You need to be smart, but not a genius." The disastrous implosion of so many 'toxic assets'[14] in the last few years eloquently supports this. These were created by highly

---

[14] A term from the noughties particularly associated with the Global Financial Crisis, it describes certain financial assets that became virtually unsaleable. These included complex structured products backed by US sub-prime mortgages, credit cards, or other types of loan. Demand in these markets collapsed when poorer mortgage borrowers began to default in large numbers and the US housing market crisis spread to other parts of the economy.

qualified people using incredibly detailed spreadsheets. However, the real world proved to be far harder to model (as always) than the super-brains believed, and the results caused substantial financial distress.

"Warren Buffett certainly does not regard a lack of super-intelligence as a hindrance"

Malcolm Gladwell, in *Outliers*[15] analyses the key determinants of success. He quotes a study from the early 1990s, conducted by psychologist K. Anders Ericsson at Berlin's Academy of Music. The Academy's professors divided the violinists into three groups – the 'stars', the 'good' and the 'rest' (somewhat unfairly classified as future teachers). The analysis showed a strong positive correlation between ability and hours spent practising. This pattern was repeated in a study of pianists. The study found no occurrences of natural stars who practised very little or dedicated students who practised often but with little success. Once a basic standard had been achieved (i.e. sufficient to gain entry into the Academy), the major factor determining progress was significant amounts of practice.

Buffett's partner Charlie Munger is quite clear on what constitutes practice in investing:

> We both [he and Buffett] insist on a lot of time being available almost every day to just sit and think. That is very uncommon in American business. We read and think. So Warren and I do more reading and thinking and less doing than most people in business. We do that because we like that kind of a life.

So perhaps practice is a more than acceptable substitute for intelligence?

November 2009

---

[15] Gladwell, Malcolm, *Outliers: The Story of Success* (Penguin, 2009).

Intuition – I knew that was going to happen

Over a Christmas lunch last year a friend told me that he had purchased just one stock over the previous twelve months: BP. What's more, he added, he hadn't really conducted any research; he had simply used his 'intuition'. This interested me on a number of levels – not least of which was the attraction of making successful decisions with little work – so I nodded politely and decided to consider the concept further. It wasn't the first time I had heard mention of intuition in investment matters. Often people say, "He has a good feel for these markets", or some investors comment, "These markets feel good".

A dictionary definition of intuition is "understanding without apparent effort". It is generally bandied about in areas as diverse as sport, music, interviewing, and gambling. One common example illustrating the power of intuition covers work conducted by research psychologist Gary Klein.[16] Klein met a fire commander convinced he had extrasensory perception. He described to Klein how he and his team had encountered a fire at the back of a house and had moved into the living room to blast water on the fire, which apparently was coming from the kitchen. Despite the firefighters' best efforts, the fire worsened until the commander's 'sixth sense' told him to clear the house. As the crew reached the street, the living room floor caved in, and the crew were saved from certain death.

Having spoken to the commander it was clear to Klein that the fire commander had detected this was not a 'normal' fire. The living room was much hotter than would have been expected and the fire was much quieter than usual. This made the commander uneasy and encouraged him to evacuate the building. The fire was indeed not

---

[16] As detailed in *Bounce: The Myth of Talent and the Power of Practice* by Matthew Syed (Fourth Estate, 2011).

'normal' – it was in fact underneath the living room rather than at the end of the living room. The commander had experienced so many fires he was aware of several repeating patterns, but in this case didn't consciously recognise any. "Experienced decision makers see a different world than novices do," concludes Klein, "and what they see tells them what they should do. Ultimately, intuition is all about perception. The formal rules of decision-making are almost incidental."

Does the use of intuition always lead to successful decision-making? Does it work better in some instances than others? Is it simply the art of recognising a familiar pattern and therefore reflective of a great amount of practice in a certain field? Or is it the use of heuristics (i.e. rules of thumb) that are more often than not incorrect?

David Myers is an acknowledged expert in this field and his book, aptly titled *Intuition*,[17] summarises the many studies made in various areas. Decisions made by intuition have been tracked and measured and the conclusion is clear. To badly misquote Samuel Goldwyn, intuition is not worth the paper it's written on. Whether assessing the quality of interviewees, the likelihood of criminals re-offending, or the chance of a patient having a particular disease, the application of statistics wins hands down when compared to the intuition of an expert in the field.

For example, Myers explains that most studies of clinical diagnosis have found that clinicians have struggled to match a computer programmed to detect the symptoms that historically were most important in providing correct diagnosis. Interviews have also been compared to a control, for example, to determine the chances of a criminal reconvicting and the interviewers have been found wanting. Some of the best studies are accidental. Myers cites a college that interviewed prospective students to whittle the

---

[17] Myers, David, *Intuition: Its Powers and Perils* (Yale University Press, 2002).

applicants down to the best 150. Very late in the day, the college received extra funding and accepted an additional 50 students that had not initially been selected. The future academic performance of these two groups was monitored and there was no difference. What a great insight into the worth of interviews!

Even when shown this evidence, the intuition experts persist in highlighting areas where intuition works. For example, they say chess players don't have time to look at every single move on the board and analyse each in detail. In fact, they don't always have time to do anything other than very limited analysis, but often they are intuitively sure that a piece 'belongs' on a certain square. Experience has taught them this shortcut. However, is this enough? If it is, why do they bother calculating any moves into the future? Why don't they simply allow their intuition to guide them? With chess computers now omniscient, the debate on whether a human chess player with his intuition is superior to an emotionless super-rational computer appears to be over.

Ex-World Chess Champion Garry Kasparov dedicates a (short) chapter to intuition in his book *How Life Imitates Chess*.[18] Kasparov, a chess romantic (in complete contrast to his arch enemy and calculating supremo Anatoly Karpov) is convinced there is something to intuition. However, he admits, it is quite hard to pin it down. He quotes the one-time head of the Spanish royal household Sabino Fernández Campo: "What I can tell you is not interesting and what is interesting I cannot tell you."

Kasparov has studied the games of all the World Chess Champions along with both the contemporaneous and modern day commentary of the matches. He is intrigued that a great deal of the commentary is incorrect and surmises that the more hurried and better moves played in these world championship games owed much to heightened 'concentration and instinct'.

---

[18] Kasparov, Garry, *How Life Imitates Chess: Making the Right Moves, from the Board to the Boardroom* (Bloomsbury Publishing PLC, 2007).

As with the rest of the book, Kasparov then uses his chess experience to search for parallels in the real world. Strangely enough, with intuition he uses the internet bubble as an example. Pay attention, he says, not to those who lost everything in the bubble, but to those clever enough to play the momentum and escape before the bubble burst, "More credit should be given to the few who played it well, whose intuition told them to go in and just how long to stay in". He makes no mention of luck.

> "Intuition is simply not a good substitute for deeper analysis"

Sadly, I can find no research conducted that measures the performance of traders, portfolio managers, or anyone else claiming their 'feel' for the market is superior to the average investor. I believe these people suffer from what David Myers calls 'illusory intuition'. They are simply falling foul of numerous well-known behavioural weaknesses, such as overconfidence,[19] to convince themselves of their innate ability.

Despite Myers belief in intuition, he struggles to win the reader over. He concludes that "intuition works well in some realms, but it needs restraints and checks in others". He doesn't articulate it, but the area that appears most relevant for intuition is that where there are definite precise answers. For example, how do children realise that they should say "big red car" rather than "red big car", or when to say "how many" and not "how much"? Because it is always so and they have learned by listening. However, when there is no definite answer – who to recruit, which way a stock is going, which move to make – intuition, or if I may be juvenile, guessing, is simply not a good substitute for deeper analysis.

January 2011

---

[19] See also 'Overconfidence? – No, I'm just right, I'm sure' (page 130).

"I don't know why I'm bothering. I know I'm not going to get the job."

Luck – an unlucky general

Paul Hart was sacked as the manager of Premiership football team Portsmouth in late November [2009]. His team was bottom of the table at the time, so the sacking came as no big surprise. However, the reason given for the decision was fairly original: "We can't continue to be unlucky in games we have been on top of," said Mark Jacob, the executive director of the club.

To be sacked for being unlucky strikes me as, well, rather unlucky. It suggests that the main source of Mr Jacob's HR training was Napoleon (who claimed he preferred lucky generals) and that he believes employment of a manager with 'hot hands' would be a big improvement on poor Mr Hart.

> "There is little doubt that luck is exceptionally important in the short term"

Do some people have more luck than others? Yes, clearly some do. However, the bad news for Mr Jacob is that this luck can run out at any moment, and tends to balance out in the very long term. Undoubtedly, some people, or sporting teams, have a reputation for being lucky, but statistics rarely support those beliefs. Of course, the great golfer Gary Player claimed that the harder he practised, the luckier he got.[20]

There is little doubt that luck is exceptionally important in the short term. All investors would definitely agree that performance over a single second is down to luck, not insight. They would all probably stretch to 30 seconds, a minute, two minutes, and so on. But eventually at some time interval, skill is considered of prime importance. (Interestingly enough, far more people seem to blame bad luck for nasty things that happen to them than thank good luck for helping them, so it is common to hear many more claims of an

---

[20] Not Arnold Palmer, as I mistakenly wrote in my original monthly commentary.

unlucky year than a lucky one.) Perhaps this period is a day, a week, a month, a quarter, a year, or even longer. The fund management environment is not particularly conducive to recognising this. Writing to my clients to tell them of an unlucky month will not impress them. Highlighting some random reasons for underperformance appears to lend it more credibility.

To identify luck's presence in an activity, Michael Mauboussin, Chief Investment Strategist of Legg Mason Capital Management, analyses how difficult it is to purposely lose. It is impossible to lose on purpose when tossing a coin, but very easy to lose at chess. How easy is it to lose at investing? I would find it hard to select a portfolio guaranteed to underperform the market over six months, one year, or even three years. Therefore, by Mauboussin's definition, there is a significant amount of luck even over periods that most investors would regard as long term.[21]

There is no obvious solution to identifying the split that exists between luck and skill, particularly as the mix changes continually. Maybe legendary Australian cricketer and cricket commentator Richie Benaud nailed it when he said: "Captaincy is 90% luck and 10% skill. But don't try it without that 10%."

Given that luck is so important, is it possible to benefit from it without unduly increasing risk? We think it is. By studying various scenarios of the future, in preference to making one forecast, one can highlight those situations where it is possible to be on the right end of a 'multi-bagger', while not putting too much at risk if the desired scenario doesn't unfold. This is analogous to betting on a horse at 50 to 1 odds when the odds should have been 5 to 1.

December 2009

---

[21] Mauboussin, Michael J., *Think Twice: Harnessing the Power of Counterintuition* (Harvard Business School, 2009).

Scepticism – 'Gullible? Me?'

Most professional investors claim to be investment sceptics. After all, no one would wish to portray themselves as a gullible buffoon. But when challenged to define individual brands of scepticism, their responses tend to be unfocused. Many would point to their interaction with management teams and boast of their talent in separating the saints from the snake oil salesmen. However, research concludes that none of us, including so-called experts, have particularly sophisticated talents in this area.

If we are devoid of the skills necessary to identify the good guys, what are the alternative ways to confidently value a company? Some suggest applying 'deep thought' or 'gut feel' to assess the credibility of various long-term forecasts. On my desk I have investment bank research documents on BT and GlaxoSmithKline. The BT note details the number of broadband subscribers the author expects in 2020, while the GlaxoSmithKline one forecasts the expected five-year sales levels from drugs in development or awaiting regulatory approval. No reader (or writer) of these notes can have confidence in these forecasts and providing he treats them with scorn, an investor can convince himself that his sceptical claims are intact. That said, it is unclear how his lack of scepticism on the forecasts that he chooses to accept can be justified. A form of selective scepticism seems to be at work here.

Dealing with forecasts is inevitably tricky, but how carefully should historical information be treated? Obviously, the highest quality information is provided in an audited set of reports and accounts – the numbers rather than the words. Occasionally, these may be less than wholly accurate, but more likely criticisms will be of insufficient detail or aggressive accounting policies.[22] Of course, once one starts wondering about transparent accounting policies, it

---

[22] See also 'Where's the potato?' (page 90) for my thoughts on accounting policies.

is logical to be suspicious of policies applied beneath the surface. After all, report and accounts are a top level summary of the application of many unseen policies.

Investors often attend company meetings to supplement the information in report and accounts. This environment provides plenty of worries for the sceptic. Company management, whilst not necessarily mendacious, may prefer to answer difficult questions with 'approximations' or semantics. The chief executive of one horrifyingly disappointing company told us we hadn't asked quite the right question before investing. Others that promised to come back to us were never heard from again. In the audit-free environment of a presentation, a company may claim ever increasing sales per square foot or growing like-for-like sales (a measure of how sales have increased on the same set of assets, usually stores, over a certain time period). Yet these terms have no strict definitions and the method of calculation can be changed at will, limiting the use of a long-term data series and invalidating comparisons between companies.

Sometimes company management is unavailable for comment and investors' questions are passed on to the investor relations team. These knowledgeable, enthusiastic, and articulate folk offer useful insights, but it should always be remembered who pays their wages.

At other times, potential investors are provided with data from surveys of industry participants or customer attitudes. However, companies may withdraw from industry surveys to avoid providing competitors with useful information or they may simply exaggerate or lie. Clever wording in a survey can lead customers into predictable responses. And while respondents may claim they will act in a particular way in a hypothetical situation, they may choose a different course of action when the event materialises. For example, private investors will typically say they buy more shares in a falling stock market, but experience shows they tend to sell.

So a true sceptic views audited figures with suspicion, ignores all non-audited historical data, and dismisses all estimates of the future as guesswork. This paints a fairly murky picture for anyone wishing to determine the merits of a share. However, one additional and very important variable must be considered: the price at which the stock can be purchased. A high price (i.e. a high valuation) suggests (growth) investors are displaying little scepticism and assuming prospects are positive, whereas a low valuation indicates a fairly downbeat – sceptical – assessment of the future is currently discounted in the price. This is one of the lovely things about purchasing shares with a margin of safety; it is not necessary to announce in advance how the margin might be used. It is available, as necessary, for mistakes, oversights, ignorance, excessive optimism, or bad luck. And if none of these occur, there is a good chance the margin of safety evolves into a profit.

Much of this commentary has emphasised the merits of scepticism to ensure investors avoid excessive bullishness in the good times. Howard Marks, a founder of Oaktree Capital Management, which manages over $80 billion in fixed interest assets, has published *The Most Important Thing*,[23] bringing together the edited highlights of his quarterly commentaries over two decades. An interesting observation he makes is, "Scepticism is usually thought to consist of saying, 'no, that's too good to be true' at the right times ... sometimes scepticism requires us to say, 'no, that's too bad to be true'". This is certainly just as important. After all, it is at these moments that one can lock in the best future returns. Investors need to be alert to pendulums swinging excessively in both directions and be prepared to act however uncomfortable the feeling.

A colleague recently suggested that scepticism is a state of mind and not a subject that can be boiled down into a 'ten easy steps' summary. I am sure he is at least half-right – a decent starting point for a sceptic.

May 2011

---

[23] Marks, Howard, *The Most Important Thing: Uncommon Sense for the Thoughtful Investor* (Columbia University Press, 2011).

Patience – as long as it takes

Conventional wisdom states that an investor only accepts risk if he is suitably rewarded. Followers of equities over the last decade (or two decades if they have been in the Japanese market) at the minimum know that 'over the very long term' is a necessary addendum to that claim. Providing 'the very long term' is never defined, we cannot really prove or disprove the statement. The investment textbooks explain this theory a touch differently, suggesting that an investor would only wish to invest in equities over bonds if he is fully compensated for the expected risk. This may be true – assuming the investor is pretty rational – but is ultimately useless unless he can correctly predict the riskiness of different asset classes or stocks.

So if we are not rewarded for taking risks, what are we rewarded for? We believe over the long term an investor is generously rewarded for patience. The great attraction of patience is that one doesn't need to be highly qualified or particularly cerebral to apply it. In fact, sitting on one's hands should be fairly easy.

For most of us, however, that isn't the case. Even in our social lives we need to read an email or text message on arrival, play with the remote control through advert breaks, or even buy a digital video recorder to eliminate the breaks altogether!

The application of patience in the stock market is no easier. We are encouraged by the huge amount of information available in the modern era to consider ourselves fully informed and therefore in a position to make high quality judgements. Most of this 'information' is marginal at best and more probably just noise and babble. To ignore it can, however, make one appear ill-informed, ignorant or at risk of being labelled as 'out of touch with the market'.

What's more, patience leads to inactivity. And that doesn't sound good to observers. When Mrs Mundy asks, "What did you do at work today, darling?" and I reply, "Nothing" it is not an exchange that typically elicits a feeling of pride or sympathy. And doing nothing in the face of much activity is also very difficult. The investor who does not react to a plummeting share price, a resignation of a previously respected management team or a dividend cut may appear to be paralysed by the news or be considered too wishy-washy to lift their backside off the fence. But few decisions are genuinely black and white. The stock market provides another barrier (even after having reached a firm decision about a company) whereby one must then decide whether other investors have already discounted that view in the share price.

The final hurdle to patient investing is the demands from third parties that blur the exercise. In an industry that calculates performance over infinitesimally small time periods, investors may act to please their masters (whether they be clients or employers). Persuading a client that performance is not great, but that the long-term future is bright is never easy. To persuade them that improvement is likely despite the inaction can be very difficult.

How patient are we and how do we make it easier to be patient?

Our average holding period for a stock is three years in comparison to an industry holding period that some sources suggest is as short as six to nine months. This holding period determines that we purchase approximately one new stock each month. As a team, we spend about 1000 hours a month evaluating and discussing ideas. On the back of that, we make one decision (which probably only took about 5% to 10% of that time). In some people's eyes this equates to an extraordinary amount of time wasted. To us, however, it is the necessary time spent analysing potential ideas (and even then some purchases may ultimately be duds). To date, we have not found a shortcut.

We are not immune to a desire for more activity. However, history reminds us that share prices can underperform for many years before

"Doing nothing in the face of much activity is very difficult"

47

bottoming, and may rise for many years afterwards. We also have a disciplined process, which generally deflects us from the noisier parts of the market. And, finally, we have (hopefully) clearly articulated our process to our clients, who understand that the chasing of short-term gains will usually have negative effects on long-term performance.

June 2009

Errors – check the checklist

My first role in the city was as a gilt analyst. Despite the exciting title, the job wasn't everything it was cracked up to be and much of my responsibility was to find anomaly switches – trades between two similar gilts that offered an arbitrage because their normal relationship had temporarily changed. One Friday afternoon I discovered an interesting (sic) switch and persuaded my boss to deal. We were actually dealing on **his** boss's fund. **Superboss** managed his fund in what is best characterised as a 'hands off' way and so, having quickly checked the previous day's print-out of the portfolio, we conducted a very large switch.

About twenty minutes after completing the transaction, and just as I was preparing to head home, we received a phone call from our settlements team. They were puzzled that we were selling a gilt that, according to their records, we didn't own. Minutes later the puzzle was solved. Superboss had completed his 'once a year' deal **the previous day** and had sold the very gilt we wished to sell **now**. Despite our Olympic-standard begging and scraping, the broker refused to cancel the deal, claiming they had already sold on the gilt we had mistakenly sold to them. Instead, they offered to release us from our duty to deliver the gilt we didn't own and asked us to deliver two other similar gilts we did own. (This formed my introduction to 'butterfly switches', a term I am unlikely to forget given the stress that accompanied my education.)

Given Superboss's passive approach to fund management, he never discovered the dealing disaster[24] and the inauspicious terms on which it was transacted discouraged me from checking the ultimate profitability of the butterfly switch.

I hadn't thought about this formative experience for some time, but was reminded of it when reading *The Checklist Manifesto* by Atul

---

[24] Until perhaps now.

Gawande.[25] Checklists have been used in aviation for many years and are credited with the significant reduction in airline accidents. History informs us that when under great pressure, and despite their intensive training, pilots can miss some very obvious and important safety steps. Consequently, checklists exist to cope with various procedures (be they take-off, landing, or mid-air emergencies). Gawande, a surgeon turned journalist, is fascinated by the potential benefits of medical checklists. In fact, he helped the World Health Organization to introduce them in a worldwide study. As medical error is estimated to be the eighth biggest killer in the US (doctors kill far more people than guns), Gawande is convinced that checklists can eliminate tens of thousands of mistakes made during surgery. Gawande highlights that error rates can be improved by placing some basic procedures on the checklist. Many items are laughably simple, ranging from confirming the surgeon is operating on the right person and the correct limb or organ, to ensuring the medical team carrying out surgery are on first name terms, that surgeons wash their hands, and so on.

Once Gawande started to look for checklists he found them in the strangest of places. None was stranger than that in the contract of rocker David Lee Roth of Van Halen, which stated that ahead of concerts the concert organiser provide a backstage serving of M&Ms with the **brown sweets removed**. These were not the weird demands of a prima donna; Mr Roth's requests were a very important part of a long document ensuring that the detailed job of building a temporary stage was not taken lightly. The M&Ms clause was embedded in the middle of the contract so the omission of the sweets was a good indicator that the checklist had been ignored – and triggered concert cancellation with full compensation to the band.

---

[25] Gawande, Atul, *The Checklist Manifesto: How to Get Things Right* (Metropolitan Books, 2009).

Gawande quotes two professors who study the science of complexity, Brenda Zimmerman of York University and Sholom Glouberman of the University of Toronto. They highlight three different types of problems. The first are **simple problems** – like recipes, these problems are effectively administrative (there's a line to make Mrs Mundy wince). Follow the rules and everything will be alright. The second type are **complicated problems**; these may be procedures initially difficult to establish, but **once** completed are easier to replicate. The professors provide the example of flying a rocket to the moon. The third type are **complex problems**; raising a child, for example. There is no set of rules, however detailed, that are guaranteed to produce a perfect outcome.

My gilt error could have been avoided with a simple checklist ("before placing a sale, always ensure you have checked electronically that the gilt is owned") and some years later Gawande discovered three fund managers who actively used checklists. The highest profile of the three was Mohnish Pabrai. Pabrai is the managing partner of Pabrai Investment Funds, "an investment group modelled after the original 1950s Buffett Partnerships". So successful was this modelling that performance was excellent for a number of years, thus encouraging Pabrai to share his secrets in his book *The Dhandho Investor*. Hubris is a wonderful thing and Pabrai's performance blew up shortly after the book's publication.[26] Pabrai, in search of a change in luck, happened across a newspaper article by Gawande and embraced an eighty-point proprietary checklist system, something that he now promotes evangelically. Sure, his performance has improved since the market bottom, but he is not alone there!

It is unclear how much checklists assist fund managers. At best, the due diligence process ensures that obvious bases are covered, and possibly significantly reduces the risk of making a stupid mistake

---

[26] And serves as a warning to all of us.

twice. One of Gawande's other evangelists suggests that it allows a fund manager to improve his outcome with no increase in skill.

"Most mistakes made in asset management are the result of complex rather than simple problems"

Most mistakes made in asset management are the result of complex rather than simple problems. Buying a stock that subsequently falls can occur for a variety of reasons. Unfortunately, a checklist that protects us from these mistakes cannot be easily created. Obviously, we can study previous errors, but it is sometimes hard to separate the relevant details from the red herrings. For example, we may have incorrectly avoided selling a share despite a director's sales, but is that a consistently good indicator? Similarly, a mistake may be blamed on ignoring excessive director remuneration, high levels of debt, and dubious accounting methods when only one (or none!) might be relevant. Checklists definitely offer some positives to an investor, but, as the perfect investment will never exist, they also risk triggering fund manager paralysis.

February 2011

3.

Fancy a Crunchie?

The Relentless Quest for Value

Fancy a Crunchie? Not at that price

Flying back into London City Airport a few minutes earlier than expected last week provided an opportunity to slip into WHSmith while I waited for Tony the Cabbie to arrive. This was not a desperate rush for a sugar fix, but a chance to conduct what, at a stretch, could be labelled primary research. I have always been fascinated by quite how much WHSmith charges for impulse items such as sweets and drinks in their travel outlets based at railway stations, airports, motorway service stations, and, more recently, hospitals. Most customers at these outlets are rushed, stressed, or captive (sometimes all three) and are therefore likely to be far less price sensitive than the typical consumer.

My analysis was not exhaustive or particularly detailed; Tony had arrived so I did not have time to buy an outrageously priced bottle of Buxton Water, but I certainly gained a flavour of WHSmith's pricing strategy. Here are the details that I noted. I have compared the prices (price 1) with those available on the Tesco website (2) and also with a local City sweetshop[27] (3):

	1	2	3
Crunchie	79p	55p	65p
Cadbury Flake	79p	56p	65p
Rice Krispies Square	109p	50p	60p
Cadbury Double Decker	79p	53p	65p
Cadbury Dairy Milk	79p	56p	65p
Starburst Smoothies Stick	79p	42p	55p

---

[27] Despite the premium prices the sweetshop charged relative to Tesco, it has now closed down, presumably unable to operate profitably under the weight of City rents and rates.

"Opportunities to benefit from latent pricing power are rare and perhaps only a handful of examples will arise over a career"

I do resent paying £1.09 for a Rice Krispies Square, particularly as my daughter can make a likeable copy for about 3p, but I also applaud WHSmith's management for turning the screw. Providing punters will pay, price maximisation must be the correct strategy. Interestingly, the company's management does not discuss this strategy explicitly in any detail when explaining its increased profitability, preferring to highlight cost-cutting, promotional activity, improving mix of products sold, and gross margin improvements. (To the reader, this could mean they are buying sweets cheaper from the manufacturers **or** charging customers more for them.) WHSmith's shares have performed well over the last five years and it is of no great surprise (sadly, in my case, with hindsight) that the company has emphasised the expansion of travel outlets in that period, growing from 129 to 532 outlets since August 2006, as compared to their high street stores, which have fallen in number from 581 to 532 over the same period.

While attempting to pay Tony the Cabbie in kind by showering him with Crunchies and Tic Tacs (£1.55!), I explained my findings to him. He was, to say the least, unimpressed by my findings, as charging premium prices to customers is not a new strategy. Of course he is correct, but it is vitally important to an investor if he can find companies that have not maximised their pricing power. Tobacco companies have unearthed great pricing power in the last decade (to the benefits of their shareholders), as have football clubs (to the benefit of their players), and the likes of Ryanair have achieved it in more underhand ways by charging ancillary fees (type in 'Cheap Flights by Fascinating Aida' on YouTube for a hilarious exposition of this).

Sadly for investors, opportunities to benefit from latent pricing power are rare and perhaps only a handful of examples will arise over a career. However, they can turbo-charge an investment in such a way that their impact on a portfolio can be extreme. Warren Buffett's purchase of See's Candy in 1972 is often used as a classic case study of the extraordinary effects of latent pricing power. Buffett has described such opportunities as being when it is possible to raise prices "rather easily without fear of significant loss of either market share or unit volume".

I left Tony with a Double Decker stuffed in his mouth and a quizzical look on his face. I assume, like me, he was in deep thought about where to find the next underpriced product.

August 2011

"Are you sure you haven't got
a vacancy for a confectionery
analyst Alastair?"

The perfect stock

A client recently highlighted a common theme raised by the fund managers he speaks to: each dedicated to buying 'good companies, with strong market shares, durable recurring earnings and high barriers to entry, particularly focused on emerging economies for their growth prospects, generating strong cash flow, run by an able management team, and available at an attractive price'. He asked me to find the weakness in that argument.

While hardly in the *Challenge Anneka*[28] category it was definitely a task that caught my imagination. My first thought was that such perfect stocks are **never** available at a **truly attractive price**. As beauty is in the eye of the beholder, an 'attractive price' is a term that an investor determined to find investment paradise can flex at will. Perhaps we should challenge such investors to tell us what price they **wouldn't** consider attractive. The narrative they create is generally strong enough to build their conviction that the price is right and that the stock will 'grow into its rating'.

Let's study the other characteristics of our nirvana stock. Market shares can always be high if defined sufficiently tightly. 'We have the largest share of pink alcopops selling in

> "'Attractive price' is a term that an investor determined to find investment paradise can flex at will"

transsexual[29] bars in Derby on a Friday night' isn't a line I have seen (yet), but is a concept I have often seen used. Similarly, while a number of companies highlight their solid base of recurring

---

[28] *Challenge Anneka* was a BBC TV programme in the 1990s in which well-known TV personality Anneka Rice was given a task to complete over a period of days. She usually succeeded by enlisting the help of unsuspecting passers-by and pleading with some companies for sponsorship of the project.

[29] See also 'The Audience Fights Back – From: Annie in Marketing' (page 183).

earnings, these often represent far less than 100% of the companies' cash earnings. For example, some investors might claim UK water companies have such characteristics, but because the regulator forces the companies to reinvest these recurring earnings into high levels of capital expenditure shareholders do not necessarily benefit.

'Barriers to entry' is a term tossed around enthusiastically by investors and is an attractive concept. However, few businesses have both good barriers to entry and strong growth prospects. For example, there's only one Man United (as the song says), which is clearly an attractive proposition, but limits growth in certain ways. Other companies may have more meaningful barriers to entry through economies of scale, but generally these businesses are regulated to protect the companies' clients from monopolistic pricing. And sometimes a barrier to entry, even if it is a local monopoly, is simply insufficient. See Plymouth Argyle for details.[30]

Emerging market growth is in demand for obvious reasons, but is not always as rewarding as it seems. A company may sell its widgets into a very large market such as China, but if there are many competitors selling similar widgets, then the size of the market must be adjusted for the size of the competition and the risk of price wars. Of course, the key assumption for emerging market economies is that they will generate superior earnings growth to Western economies. However, if too much capital is invested in these markets, profitability may disappoint overall (and maybe if Western economies are starved of capital, some other areas could surprise on the upside).

Cash flow has many definitions – and investors often use the measure that most aids their valuation argument. If cash before

---

[30] Plymouth Argyle Football Club play in League Two of the Football League (the fourth highest division in English football). Despite its location in the south-west of England, an area not renowned as a hotbed of professional football and thus lacking in much competition, Argyle average a home crowd of only 8,000.

capital expenditure, dividends, interest, tax, and all those other unhelpful items is the most attractive, then that calculation is favoured. Compared to twenty years ago, cash flow typically is fairly

> **"Few businesses have both good barriers to entry and strong growth prospects"**

close to profits and so adds little to the argument. Because of declining cigarette volumes, tobacco companies have limited capital expenditure needs and have truly attractive cash flow relative to profits after taking off **all** the horrible stuff – but the list of such stocks is, however, pretty short.

We have covered the assessment of management teams often.[31] In summary, we struggle to separate luck from skill and assume that most management teams are of average ability. We definitely refuse to pay up for a management team perceived as superior to its peers.

If large numbers of investors are chasing after the same type of stock, it suggests there is another type with a diminishing band of followers. Our favourites in this category are those stocks that, given their sensitivity to the economic cycle, are classic downgrade candidates, but which we believe have excellent long-term prospects. These stocks have no catalysts, no stories and, in many investors' eyes, no future. Sounds perfect.

November 2010

---

[31] Although this statement is chronologically correct, commentaries appertaining to management quality and our ability to spot it are grouped together in chapter four.

Falling knives I – have you lost your nerve?

Discussion of our contrarian principles over many years leaves some of our clients rather surprised to find that we are not knee-deep in the many horrific performers of 2008. Have we lost our nerve? Do we just talk a good game? Or is something else holding us back?

While we have always argued that it is correct, in general, to catch falling knives, we know that some knives can do serious damage. Over the long term, however, a strategy of buying underperforming shares has typically paid dividends, as investors have overestimated the default risk in individual companies. Until recently few large companies had gone bust, because in the good times there are plenty of escape plans, such as new management or corporate activity. But in the last year there have been a number of failures or near failures, such as Northern Rock, Bradford & Bingley, Woolworths, and New Star Asset Management. It has been incredible to watch the speed of decline; very difficult trading conditions have interacted with appalling banking conditions. Therefore, apparently, we have transitioned into a period where investors (including ourselves in some stocks) have been underestimating the risk of default.

So what strategy have we employed to accept more risk on the portfolio? Typically, the companies that enter our universe (usually extreme underperformers) have up to four problems – cyclical risk, structural risk (perceived or real), balance sheet risk, and specific risk (for example, a company that is struggling even if its industry is not). Usually, the greater the number of problems, the higher the risk the company represents. For example, the retailer Woolworths was under great structural pressure from the supermarkets, cyclical pressure as consumer spending weakened, balance sheet pressure as the management devised increasingly complex financing arrangements, and finally specific pressure as, for example, it struggled to move sufficient product from the stock room to the store shelves.

It is obviously wrong to be too prescriptive in our approach. In general, though, in 2008 we have focused on those underperformers with perhaps just one or two of these problems rather than a full suite. For example, customers of the pub retailer J D Wetherspoon are under financial pressure currently, but the company does have the biggest and busiest pubs, strong cash flow relative to stated profits, and a 'value' offering. We believe that rival Punch Taverns has much greater problems because of its complex financing and much smaller (and less competitive) pubs.

The high rate of technological change in society continues to exert great pressure on a number of businesses. For example, what will the relevance be of local or national newspapers, DVDs, physical retailers of electrical products and telephone directories in ten years' time? Furthermore, are the current incumbents well-placed to benefit from and adapt to changes to their industries or will the most recent competitors be nimbler? We also question whether the elongated credit boom has allowed businesses to prosper over the last 15 years and if future conditions will be less auspicious. For example, how sure are we that demand for first-class air travel, foreign weekend breaks, buy-to-let mortgages, and expensive cars will return soon?

A number of investors are currently avoiding reasonably or highly indebted companies irrespective of their long-term prospects. While we understand this, we believe there are some cheap companies that can continue servicing their debt, albeit at a higher cost, before ultimately generating a much higher level of profits than today. Perhaps we have underestimated the specific risk of default on this group of stocks, but as a sub-portfolio we believe the overall long-term returns should be very good.

November 2008

Falling knives II – dealing with the losers

My wife recently gave me a final warning about the scale of my book purchases from Amazon. Her heightened disciplinary actions are apparently based on health and safety issues rather than on financial or educational concerns. She was worried that the 'book mountain' next to our bed could collapse and endanger the limbs of small children who might be in the vicinity. Somewhat aggrieved by this, and eager to escape an outright ban, I conducted an audit of the Mundy family library aiming to complete a small cull.

What quickly became clear was my predilection for 'How To' books. Many sports and pastimes are covered: snooker, badminton, cricket, tennis, chess, table tennis, and even backgammon. A psychoanalyst would probably have a field day, detecting someone striving for perfection (actually, I would be pretty happy to lift my standard in most of these pursuits to mediocre). My investment library[32] mirrors the theme and holds several 'How To' books by a number of 'greats' plus a few written by some 'never was-es'. I was struck while studying these investment books that they emphasised buying rather than selling skills.

This is similar to fund manager presentations that articulate an investment process, and particularly the buying discipline, in minute detail, but limit comments on the selling discipline to a bare minimum, typically explaining that sales occur when shares hit fair value. This discipline no doubt works well for successful stock picks, but can it be as easily applied to the losers?

These losers are generally termed 'value traps'. In the last few years, many shares in ordinary looking companies have fallen precipitously. For example, Royal Bank of Scotland, Enterprise Inns,

---

[32] See 'Further Reading – Build Your Own Book Mountain' (page 185).

Dixons Retail, Trinity Mirror, Premier Foods, and Yell amongst others have fallen more than 90% from highs reached in the past five years. It is clearly essential to avoid such dogs.

Most value investors will generally assess a company's long-term earnings prospects when valuing its shares, believing this creates an edge over the crowd. The average investor – the market – usually operates on a far shorter time horizon than value investors and, therefore, disappointing company earnings are often accompanied by a falling share price. This gives value investors an opportunity to average down, providing the assessment of the company's long-term earnings power is unchanged and produces a share price well in excess of the current depressed levels. This process is fine if the falling share eventually reverses and morphs into a winner, but how does the value investor remain sufficiently objective and flexible to capitulate if necessary?

There are some straightforward mechanistic ways of dealing with losers, such as implementing a stop-loss or reacting to a broken support line on a chart. But value investors have little confidence in selling a share simply because it is falling and would certainly not categorise such decisions as objective.

One approach that can work, even in markets where information is disseminated widely, is to emphasise the importance of a company's balance sheet in preference to the market's focus on the profit and loss account. Sometimes the long-term future of a company may appear bright, but the company's balance sheet might be too weak to guarantee its future. Short-term investors are so fixated on earnings trends rather than balance sheet risk that they may underestimate bankruptcy risk.

An alternative defence against the dogs is to sell when the original thesis for buying the shares no longer holds. For example, a change in regulation may reduce the long-term earnings power of a company and therefore demand the investor reassess his hypothesis and sell his shares. However, this news is often reflected immediately in the share price, so while the original (pre-regulation) story may no longer hold, the shares may have become even cheaper relative to the reduced level of long-term earnings. While some investors use this selling method, they must be very clear in their rationale for the initial investment and be comfortable selling 'cheap' shares when the story changes.

Some painful losses can be avoided by greater awareness of the type of stocks that land one in trouble. A useful investing tool is to maintain an audit of one's decisions. If there are identifiable trends in that audit, it is sensible to take heed of them. For example, such an audit informed us that we typically generate superior performance in mid and large cap stocks and not small caps. Consequently, we now concentrate our efforts away from the tiddlers.

> "Some painful losses can be avoided by greater awareness of the type of stocks that land one in trouble"

One other area we are increasingly aware of when analysing a stock is the assessment of bankruptcy risk. ('Bankruptcy risk' is used here as shorthand to mean the likelihood of shares falling very significantly and permanently from their current levels. Bankruptcy itself may not happen or may only happen years later. Whether it does or not, the company is unlikely to regain its former glories.) I think most investors asked five years ago to assess the bankruptcy risk of the companies mentioned earlier would have severely underestimated the odds. However, even though five years seems far into the distance, a value investor who prefers not to sell on the way down (as the 'value' will if anything be greater) needs to accept that this is within his investment horizon and must attach some probability of default risk into his analysis. When we analysed

Thomas Cook in 2010 the balance sheet concerned us, not for any immediate reason, but simply because the company operates in a volatile industry and the balance sheet was inappropriate relative to the industry's characteristics.

Analysing default risk is clearly as much an art as a science, but the list of stocks referenced earlier provides some indications of where risks are greatest. First and foremost, high levels of debt in all their various guises can be highly dangerous. Secondly, technological obsolescence can be very significant, and thirdly, some products and services can undoubtedly slip into long-term structural decline. Conditions can deteriorate exponentially if debt is combined with either of the other two factors. While this extra information can indicate heightened risk, we cannot expect to calculate an exact probability of that risk. That said, experience has taught us that the probability is often significantly higher than it appears at the original time of analysis. *Caveat emptor.*

July 2011

"It's lovely when the
kids sleep in."

What's the catalyst?

Often during meetings with clients and prospective clients, I am encouraged to justify one or two of our holdings. Typically, I try to provide an impassioned defence of the investment with a few erudite thoughts detailing the stock's many qualities – there's no harm in aiming high after all. Clients usually sit there politely and sometimes even feel duty bound to take a note. More often than not they then enquire what the catalyst will be to crystallise this value.

If an investor **really** wants to buy a stock it is always possible to find a catalyst: new management, a potential bid, forthcoming results, the implementation of a share buy-back, and so on. Once identified, the alleged catalyst imbues the stock with powers so special that many investors are convinced they need no protective equipment, such as a strong balance sheet or good cash flow. Dangerously, potential negatives are brushed aside as the upcoming catalyst takes star billing.

Let's imagine a large retailer that has suffered a poor trading period and has an uncomfortable level of debt. A new management team is appointed and subsequently provides a strategy update. Management is delighted to announce the successful test marketing of three 'new-style' stores. The success encourages them to roll out the 'new style' across the remaining 918 stores, at significant cost. Investors are encouraged to extrapolate the marvellous results (which have probably been hideously over-costed, implemented by the company's best people, and contain numbers calculated in the best light) across the whole estate to calculate the potential for higher profits. The catalyst is clearly the roll-out of the new-style stores, but the risk is that the other stores perform less impressively than the first three stores; the refurbishments achieve only a transitioning of the company's debt position from very poor to terrible and cause a substantial share price fall.

"There is just one catalyst we have found that works well"

For the investor betting on the catalyst it is essential that the refurbishments work, as failure will likely result in heavy losses. This is fine as catalyst hunters do not usually suffer significant fears of failure. As contrarian investors we, instead, search for a margin of safety and seek to avoid drinking in the last chance saloon. Is it not better to be invested in a similar company – but one that has a stronger balance sheet? We can then wait patiently for a management team to turn the company around without second-guessing in advance which management team will succeed.

We live in an instant world – everyone wants performance now[33] – and the search for, and belief in, catalysts encourages investors and their clients to believe they are in charge of their own destiny. There is no evidence whatsoever that those catalyst-hunters perform better in the short term. Interestingly, there is just one catalyst we have found that works well, albeit not on a timescale that is necessarily attractive to short-term investors, and that is: low valuations.

April 2011

---

[33] My favourite story about a catalyst is when, after a large pharmaceutical company published its final results, an analyst at an investment bank stood up to provide his colleagues with his analysis of the company's extraordinarily detailed and comprehensive release. When he finished his presentation he asked whether there were any questions. An eager salesman raised his hand and asked 'what's the next catalyst'? Clearly in the world of catalysts it is better to travel than arrive.

Are shorters evil?

I was recently sitting on a panel at a conference at which we were asked our thoughts on stock-lending and shorting. Shorters are typically viewed as the devil incarnate – nasty people who flail around at will trying their luck by selling a company's shares to force the price down and buying back at lower prices. I think that is incredibly unfair. A shorter needs nerves of steel as his potential loss is unlimited.[34] His analysis must be of the highest quality and his timing must be spot on too. Just think of all the value bears in the late 1990s who lost significant sums in the Technology, Media and Telecommunications (TMT) bull market because they were too early rather than wrong.

Having made an impassioned defence of the shorting fraternity, I further antagonised my fellow panellists by declaring I was quite happy in most circumstances to

> "A shorter is a long-term investor's friend"

lend stock to a shorter so he could sell my stock.[35] My argument was simple. Yes, a shorter may force a share price down, but surely that provides an investor with an opportunity to buy a stock at an even lower price than he had achieved previously. I felt it was an excellent example of sacrificing short-term performance with the aim of maximising long-term performance. I'm not convinced I won the audience over, but I stick with my view that a shorter is a long-term investor's friend.

June 2011

---

[34] Not much has been written on shorting, but two great books on the subject are *Fooling Some of the People All of the Time: A Long Short Story* by David Einhorn (John Wiley & Sons, 2008) and *Confidence Game: How a Hedge Fund Manager Called Wall Street's Bluff* by Christine S Richard (John Wiley & Sons, 2010).

[35] I do agree that sometimes stock lending is dumb. For example, lending stock in bank shares to shorters can result in a falling share price, which can itself generate a lack of confidence amongst customers and, at worst, a run on the bank.

Correlations – not so simple

An investor borrowing Doctor Who's TARDIS[36] in 1998 and travelling to 2008 to gain some investment insight would have been surprised by a number of changes (not least the election of Boris Johnson as Mayor of London). Perhaps one of the big price changes apparent would be the price increase of a barrel of oil from about US$10 to approximately $125. If our intrepid explorer then returned to 1998 and wished to buy a share benefiting from this theme, BP would have appeared a sensible pick. He would, however, have been disappointed. Between 1998 and 2008, and despite the strength of the oil price, BP is virtually unchanged both in absolute terms and relative to the FTSE All-Share Index.

April 2008

---

[36] Time and Relative Dimension in Space. According to Wikipedia, a properly maintained and piloted TARDIS can transport its occupants to any point in time and any place in the universe.

Large cap investing – does size matter?

After yet another year of mid caps comfortably outperforming large caps, I assume it will not be long before we read some obituaries of the FTSE 100. Some chochem[37] will explain how blindingly obvious it is that the largest companies are at a disadvantage. After all, they will say, they cannot get much larger because they have such big market shares and, in fact, are highly vulnerable as smaller competitors snap away at their ankles using more flexible, guerrilla-like strategies to increase their market positions.

One apparently strong piece of empirical evidence that the obituary writers usually offer is that many of the original constituents of stock market indices are no longer with us. This, they claim, proves that younger, faster-growing companies have replaced them and that economic progress ensures this evolution. They then support their argument by pointing out the laughably old-fashioned companies that were original constituents of the FT 30 back in 1935. After all, they will gently chide, if investing in large companies is so successful how are Patons & Baldwins, Fine Spinners and Doublers, and Callender's Cables & Construction currently trading?

Jeremy Siegel, a Professor of Finance, author and television talking head offers some interesting research in this area, detailed in his book *The Future for Investors*.[38] Siegel's study took the original

---

[37] Chochem ('kok m') is a Hebrew word literally meaning 'wise man'. However, its Yiddish use is for sarcastic/ironic purposes with 'man' being replaced with 'guy' such as 'which chochem had this idea?'. My grandma particularly enjoyed using it, but I think that was because it was one of the few Hebrew/Yiddish words she knew, rather than because she was a master of irony. See also 'The Audience Fights Back – From Mum:' (page 183).

[38] Siegel, Jeremy J., *The Future for Investors* (Crown Business, 2005). Do not take this as a book recommendation from me; I am sharing with you one of the best parts of what I found to be quite a tedious book. It was on page 78 that he lost me for good. In summarising the lessons that investors should have learned from the technology bubble he lists: "Avoid triple digit price to earnings ratios."

constituents of the S&P 500 in 1957 and followed their progress to 2003. Siegel used three approaches to compare the performance of the S&P 500 with that of the portfolios generated from the original S&P 500. First, he held all stocks provided they maintained their market listing (regardless of how small they became). Secondly, he held all stocks even if they merged. And finally, he also held all spin-offs (from demergers) so that no shares were ever sold.

Siegel found that all three of these 'descendant' portfolios outperformed the S&P 500 Index over 46 years, even though the index was continually updated with new entrants. Intuitively, this is hard to believe with fast-growing companies marching into the indices to replace those companies apparently in terminal decline. However, while it might have made a good story if all the original constituents went bust making abacuses and horse-drawn carriages, the truth is more complex. The main reasons that index constituents had changed so much was that companies broke themselves up, were bid for, changed their business focus through acquisitions or mergers, or simply changed their name. And many of these events were profitable for investors. Siegel emphasises one main factor for the outperformance – the reinvestment of high dividend yields. This factor more than overcame the lower earnings growth generated by the originals.

So being large is not as bad as portrayed. Why is that? First, perhaps larger companies identify less beneficial uses for their capital and so are happy to consistently return it to shareholders. And maybe, the companies' dividend payments act as an excellent discipline and one that provides a challenging hurdle for capital projects to beat if they are to be signed off. Compare this to a fast-growing company in a relatively new area encouraged by shareholders to invest more capital in its embryonic business. (In a separate study, Siegel found that companies with high capital expenditure to sales

"Being large is not as bad as portrayed"

ratios significantly underperformed those with low capital expenditure to sales ratios.) Evidence suggests that much of this capital is wasted.

Some industries are enormous and, therefore, the largest players are by definition large. GlaxoSmithKline has a smaller market share of the global pharmaceutical market than Topps Tiles has of the UK tile market – just because GlaxoSmithKline is a larger company does not, on its own, indicate its relative growth path. Large companies also became large and remained so because of some very important benefits that size bestows. Tesco's market strength creates great buying power, which leads to hefty profits and provides the capital to invest in the most attractive sites for new superstores. Who would wish to back a small independent food retailer to compete against Tesco?

There are many other advantages that largeness bestows, such as lower borrowing costs than competitors, better payment terms with suppliers and customers, the opportunity to spread research and development costs over a larger sales base, and economies of scale in advertising spend.

Of course, smaller and mid-sized companies sometimes succeed and generate growth through huge market share gains and/or creating new markets or sub-markets. Ryanair, easyJet, Direct Line, J D Wetherspoon, Majestic Wine, Travel Inn, and many other companies have grown spectacularly in the last 25 years or so to significant positions in their industry. I am not sure it is that easy to spot in advance those industries most susceptible to competition. The two airline companies benefited from undercutting incumbents with high and sticky costs. Direct Line built a brand on cheap advertising during a recession while introducing a 'new' method of purchase (the telephone). J D Wetherspoon was competing in the early days against brewers that regarded their pubs as secondary to their main business of brewing beer. And Majestic emphasised a particular part of the alcohol market and created a destination specialist store. These industries were perhaps ripe for new entrants, but for every J D Wetherspoon and Majestic there have been many lookalikes, such as Regent Inns and Oddbins, which either failed or fizzled out.

I would conclude, and this certainly does not justify even the smallest of drum rolls, that over sensibly long time periods, sometimes small and medium sized companies will perform well against large companies and sometimes vice versa. And the most important determinant of this outperformance is quite achingly dull: starting valuations.

December 2010

Investing in IPOs – what's not to like?

We are sometimes asked whether we participate in new issues (initial public offerings or IPOs). Historically, it is an area where we have had little exposure, mainly because of our strong views on the subject. The academic evidence on the long-term successes of IPOs is, to be generous, mixed. However, a comprehensive study of 5,821 IPOs highlighted by Loughran and Ritter in *Investment Fables* by Aswath Damodaran[39] calculated that IPO firms underperformed peers by high single digits per annum for up to four years.

The odds appear to be against the long-term investor in IPOs. The company selling its shares picks the time to sell, which suggests it has an inherent advantage over the buyer. In addition, the seller, particularly in recent times, employs a long list of well-remunerated investment banks to portray the company in as attractive a light as possible, simultaneously ensuring the number of naysayers is reduced.

So why do investors participate in IPOs? Psychologist Robert Cialdini has highlighted six weapons that salespeople use to steer buyers into decisions[40]: reciprocity (someone does something for you, so you feel you owe him), commitment (you said you would buy some and now you feel you cannot step back), authority (someone in power is telling you to do it), liking (you like the salesperson and wish to please them), scarcity (buy now while stocks last), and social proof (everyone else is doing it, so it must be okay).

Perhaps the investment banks believe they have some authority and that their clients like them. My guess is that scarcity and

---

[39] Damodaran, Aswath, *Investment Fables: Exposing the Myths of "Can't Miss" Investment Strategies* (Financial Times/Prentice Hall, 2004).

[40] Cialdini, Robert, *Influence: The Psychology of Persuasion* (HarperBusiness, 2007).

particularly social proof hold sway. It is just so embarrassing to potentially miss out on a successful trade, especially if everyone else is buying.

Added to Cialdini's weapons is the argument that investors love a good story. If an IPO is complemented with a plan for the company to grow significantly, it is more likely to appeal. Typically, the incentive for investors to participate is that they gain very early exposure to these long-term growth stories when the companies' management teams are short of capital.

Ocado is an interesting case study. It was floated on the market in July 2010 by, amongst others, Goldman Sachs. It seems fairly consensual that Ocado provides customers with a pleasant experience. They offer a host of delivery slots, arrive punctually, employ charming delivery people, deliver virtually all of the items ordered, and if they do send substitutes they do so appropriately. (Unlike my experience of Tesco – I remember some years ago, their delivery lady explaining to me that while carrots and light bulbs both help you see in the dark, "they ain't exactly substitutes are they?").[41] With broadband coverage growing and shoppers ever more relaxed about shopping online, the narrative certainly encouraged prospective investors.

However, this was no easy sell as Ocado had not made an operating profit since it began trading in 2002. The bankers employed two cunning tricks – one on price, the other on valuation. They initially announced the share price would be in an eye-watering range of 200p to 275p with a market capitalisation of well over £1 billion. However, the shares were ultimately issued at the 'bargain' price of 180p, allowing investors to pat themselves on the back for negotiating a better price.

---

[41] See also 'The Audience Fights Back – From: John' (page 182).

Valuation was a bit trickier, as it typically is for a company that has never made a profit. But when the prize is super high fees, there is no end to human ingenuity within investment banks. Unfortunately, we cannot find the original valuation work on Ocado conducted by Goldman's, but we do have a copy of their note of 31 August 2010, six weeks after flotation. In this note they compared Ocado to the highly successful Amazon (rather than to the not-quite-so-triumphant Boo.com and Webvan). However, even this leap of faith was insufficient because on Goldman's chosen valuation metric of enterprise value (EV)/sales, virtually the only valuation metric that conceivably made Ocado appear cheap, Amazon looked even cheaper.

Step forward ASOS, the UK's largest online-only fashion and beauty store, and YOOX, an Italian internet mail order retailer. Once again, a simple comparison here was inadequate as YOOX and ASOS didn't make Ocado clearly attractive. So Goldman's added one more twist. They suggested that by using the 2011 EV/sales ratios of these companies at their (Goldman's) bullish price targets rather than employing the standard convention of using current prices, then Ocado appeared to be cheap. And this cheapness they believed could drive the shares all the way back up to 200p – a whopping 10% premium to the issue price.

As both ASOS and YOOX had higher prices when Ocado floated, it is likely that a similar valuation approach was used at that time. Heaven knows how the 275p top of the range price was justified! Suffice to say, more conventional valuation measures and more appropriate competitors were given only the most perfunctory of mentions.

A year later it is revealing that much of Goldman's optimism has proved unfounded. Forecasted operating profit for the year ending November 2011 was at the time of the initiation note, £23.3 million, whereas by 11 September 2011 the same analyst was suggesting just £6.7 million. Even Goldman's current price target stands at only

"Any time anybody offers you anything with a big commission and a 200 page prospectus, don't buy it"

133p, while other analysts have targets significantly lower.[42]

Of course, Ocado is merely one example of an unsuccessful IPO for investors. The combination of over-optimistic profit forecasts and inappropriate valuation comparisons is, however, far from rare. Not surprisingly, Charlie Munger has summed it up very well and concisely, "Any time anybody offers you anything with a big commission and a 200 page prospectus, don't buy it". It's hard to argue with his conclusion.

September 2011

---

[42] When Ocado finally announced its operating profit for the year ending November 2011 it was just £1.1m.

4.

A Psycho in the Boardroom?

Quizzing Company Management

A psycho in the boardroom?

For reasons which I have now forgotten, I recently purchased a book on psychopathy. Perhaps it was because I had previously read that some studies suggest between 3% and 4% of chief executive officers (CEOs) are psychotic and thought that if I could spot the odd one or two, then it might help performance. (I am talking here about avoiding psychopaths rather than embracing them, but will return to that point later.)

Jon Ronson's *The Psychopath Test: A Journey through the Madness Industry*[43] is a merry jaunt through a complex subject. As you would expect, psychopaths are not easy to identify. In fact, there is no consensus on exactly how to define them, even amongst the professionals and experts in the field.

The test conventionally used by psychologists and associated professions is the twenty point Hare PCL-R Checklist. This list details a number of common characteristics such as superficial charm, parasitic lifestyle, impulsivity, and the failure to accept responsibility (and, yes, I too thought that described the fund management industry perfectly). The Hare Checklist generates a score out of 40. Sadly there is no precise score that defines a psychopath, although 30 is generally used as a strong indication. To further complicate the test, because psychopaths are cunning and manipulative, the examiner must be aware that they can possibly affect their score by responding to questions in a particular way.

At various times during his journey the author spends time with Bob Hare, the creator of the Checklist. Hare comments upon one area of frustration, "I shouldn't have done my research just in prisons.

---

[43] Ronson, Jon, *The Psychopath Test: A Journey through the Madness Industry* (Picador, 2011).

"The risk of a company turning rotten while psychopaths are in charge must thus be significantly increased"

I should have spent some time in the Stock Exchange as well", as he believes the corporate world is a fertile ground for psychopaths. (To be fair to him, Hare has written a book on the latter subject as well as conducting a large academic study, which supported his views.)

Why would a psychopath be comfortable in a senior corporate role? Well, CEOs often need to make tough decisions, such as the closure of factories and offices and the implementation of mass redundancies. Any normal person would surely be touched to some extent by these actions and the repercussions on those affected. But psychopaths, with their lack of remorse and empathy and failure to accept responsibility for their actions, would find these deeds much easier than most.

Is it good or bad to be invested in a company run by a psychopath? On the whole, I think it is far from optimal, but I do wonder how many of us have profited from backing CEOs who have aggressively cut costs, shrunk working capital, and managed a very tight ship. And is this really psychotic behaviour or simply excellent housekeeping? Of course, while his cost-cutting 'abilities' may be construed positively, the day-to-day management techniques of someone on the psychopathic spectrum, as I prefer to think of it, may be far from the highest quality. The risk of a company turning rotten (losing key staff and customers) while psychopaths are in charge must thus be significantly increased.

As contrarian investors we are typically faced with underperforming companies aiming to generate some sort of recovery. These companies inevitably suffer more cost-cutting than most and it is impossible as an outsider to always distinguish 'good' cost-cutting (cuts that are essential for the business to compete with its peers) or 'bad' cost-cutting (cuts that eat into the bones of the organisation), but it is usually a fair bet that the longer such cuts continue, the more desperate they become. To detect short-termism and the bullying of staff is very much harder.

So, what tactics can investors employ if they wish to sidestep the psychos? Hare proposes the candidate is shown a particularly gruesome crime scene photograph. If he is disgusted and appalled by it immediately then it is a fairly standard reaction, but Hare claims a psychopath will study the picture with unemotional curiosity. It certainly sounds like a great test, but I am pondering how to subtly introduce it into a discussion with company management that we meet.

November 2011

"...And now I'd like to introduce our new Chief Executive."

When chaff looks like wheat

I have often remarked to clients that it is very hard to accurately assess whether a company's management is exceptionally good or if they are merely smooth-talking snake oil salesmen. For example, even if the team's explanation of the company's success is plausible, they may have just taken the helm at a fortuitous time in the company's business cycle. The downfall of some previously high-flying executives, who had at their peak received knighthoods or various other honours, suggests we are not alone in struggling to consistently sort the wheat from the chaff.

But, is it any easier to identify the poor or even crooked managers? Many years ago a young investor recommended giving a wide berth to senior management who wore bow ties. (I think he was shown the door by his employers for providing what was probably pretty decent investment advice.) There have undoubtedly been numerous pub fireside conversations over the years as to whether facial hair or non-white shirts with white collars are 'risk' factors. We can find no academic studies to support these claims.

But the prize for spotting poor managers is worth winning. A number of silver-tongued chiefs have hoodwinked investors over the years and successfully talked their share prices up to rarefied levels. Investors who can avoid these stocks as they tumble back to earth can save their clients a lot of anguish.

What clues can we search for? Over the years we have monitored the share transactions of directors with interest. Large share sales are always worth investigating, particularly if accompanied by claims that they are necessary to fund extensions, swimming pools, divorces, or tax bills. However, worse than a sale is a purchase that is never made, particularly after claims that the shares are cheap

"The prize for spotting poor managers is worth winning"

(excuses often given here are 'I don't have any spare cash', 'we always seem to be restricted by our legal department' and, 'I've got enough skin in the game because I'm Chief Executive'). Even big purchases made by directors might be worth handling with care as it is possible they are desperate to create a false impression of confidence ahead of bank refinancing.

Director largesse has typically been uncovered in the media with stories of private helicopters, extraordinarily ornate expensive office décor, or in the case of one chief executive an alleged US$6,000 on shower curtains. Even if these are reliable indicators of incompetence, or worse criminality, they are challenging for an average investor to uncover. A cursory glance through the tabloids is certainly worthwhile every so often.

It is always worth investigating management's previous roles – have they a link with failing companies? Have they ever had personal financial difficulties? Obviously the internet greatly aids such 'research'. Other risk factors worth monitoring are nepotism (not always a bad thing) and transactions between the listed company and another company that share board members.

We are sceptical of managers who serially acquire other businesses. Academic research concludes that the majority of takeovers destroy value, but they do make it difficult for observers to calculate the organic growth of a company and can therefore sustain the reputation of a poor manager for longer than is warranted.

It is interesting to monitor boards of directors that have remained largely unchanged for many years. These boards may have run out of ideas, or have lost frustrated high-quality management below board level.

It is best to treat warily management who spend significant time informing shareholders of the cheapness of their company's shares as well as those who spend excessive time on PR in preference to the more mundane activity of running a company.

Meeting a management team can often help. Does the finance director appear weak or overly subservient to the chief executive? Is the same question answered consistently over time? Is the strategy constantly changing? Are accounting policies frequently altered and operating divisions often rejigged? Are the company's auditors well known? Does senior management openly admit to errors and concerns about the future, or are they always confident of reaching exacting targets? Are the non-executives cronies (or even worse, MPs)?

These warning indicators aren't comprehensive proof, but they do trigger some flashing lights and provide food for thought. Sometimes incompetents or crooks can keep balls in the air for years; however, over the long term a fund manager who avoids investing in low quality management teams surely has a greater chance of achieving long-term success.

May 2009

Accounting tricks – where's the potato?

Several years ago around Christmas time a stockbroker used to invite a few of us to a lunch at which we were entertained by Terry, a magician. Terry is brilliant. He specialises in table-top magic, where the audience is just a few inches from the magician, rather than stage magic, where trap doors and false bottoms are much harder to detect.

Every year Terry kicked off the entertainment with an excellent but simple trick. He came into the room wearing a trilby, placed it on the table and then, every now and again, raised it to reveal various items of increasing size. Our favourite part, and his final flourish, was when a huge potato suddenly appeared from beneath the hat.

Given that he was evidently up to something (illusion, distraction, etc.) I set out at an early stage to unravel the mechanics of the potato trick, but despite my commitment to this sleuth work I always lost concentration at the vital moment. I must have watched it half a dozen times before I actually saw what Terry did. I hope Terry will forgive me if I lift the lid on it – I am still in awe of the rest of his show.[44] It was a straightforward distraction trick. While he chatted amusingly to the audience and, as importantly, waved his right hand around manically, his left hand was busy removing the potato from his pocket and placing it underneath the hat. Simple, but brilliant, and the reaction of the guests over many years told its own story.

What's the relevance of Terry and his magic to this month's report? Well, it struck me recently that the management of many companies are conducting a variant of the potato trick when they

---

[44] After a few years we pleaded with Terry to show us how to do a card trick and with great patience he showed us how you can place certain cards in a pack so that they are in a perfect place from which to deal yourself a full house. He then turned over the cards to reveal a royal flush!

communicate with shareholders. Ideally they are providing us with sufficient information to assess the value of their company's shares, but sadly they usually have a conflict of interest – they need a higher share price

> "The management of many companies are conducting a variant of the potato trick when they communicate with shareholders"

to increase the value of their options. They will, therefore, do their best to distract us from any nasty areas and focus us on the good stuff. From their perspective, it is absolutely essential they keep us looking at the manic right hand so that we never see the potato.

There's no easy way around this. Management teams, like magicians, are highly skilled performers who have spent several years refining their skills. However, one way to rise above the distraction trick is to simply ask: 'Where's the potato?'

August 2010

I can assure shareholders
our accounting policies are
of the highest standard.

Remuneration – when's enough, enough?

Every so often we receive letters from the Chairmen of Remuneration Committees of companies in which we are significant shareholders. Each letter typically follows a standard format.

First, we are informed how lucky we are to have such a fine management team running the company and how very important it is that this team is sufficiently remunerated. We would, after all, hate to see the chaps demotivated or lured away by a nasty competitor. We are then encouraged to study a review of the pay and conditions of the management's peers at similar companies. Extraordinarily, these studies always illustrate that our executives are struggling along with packages that must provide them with huge embarrassment when partying the night away at industry conventions.

Of course, the Chairman of the Remuneration Committee is only too pleased to share with us his cunning plan to prevent the management team slipping into penury. His solutions are usually a pay increase and the introduction of numerous executive share schemes which, when added together, ensure that it is unlikely the recipients will ever need to grope down the back of the sofa looking for a bit of loose change. Finally, the Chairman signs off with an offer to pop round for a cup of coffee and explain in more detail everything we have just read.

We have both replied to and ignored these letters and have noticed the end result is generally the same. The Remuneration Committee has generally completed its research and made its decisions and has little interest in highly paid (did someone whisper overpaid?) portfolio managers complaining about other people lining their pockets. It is unclear whether it is apathy or passive acceptance, but we can remember only once in recent times

"I think I can spot an outrageously generous pay package"

shareholders sufficiently irate at a mooted pay deal that the majority voted against it. Even on this occasion, we were informed that the vote, as with all remuneration votes, was simply 'advisory' and that the pay deal had been implemented some months previously. Despite receiving the big thumbs down the scheme was not adjusted.[45]

However, in a perverse way, we are rather relieved to be ignored on these matters. While I think I can spot an outrageously generous pay package, I'm far less confident when forced to generate a fair and sensible alternative. I think that to prevent recipients gaming the system a bonus should cover several variables: return on capital employed, cash flow, total shareholder return, earnings per share, use of exceptional items, and so on. I would also like to see bonuses earned over the long term so that quick wins are not secured at the expense of longer-term gains and be partially deferred past the departure of a management team; this would incentivise them to find high quality replacements and to allow these replacements time to find any hidden bodies. None of this would necessarily result in lower bonuses, but it might ensure the biggest bonuses would only be paid to the most deserving cases.

Dan Ariely's new book *The Upside of Irrationality*[46] covers the issue of remuneration in a fascinating way by studying the behaviour of rats when performing under different incentivisation terms.

---

[45] There has, indeed, been greater debate on this subject since November 2010. Shareholders have become increasingly feisty when faced with pay deals they regard as excessive and a number of advisory votes have attracted a large percentage of votes against boards' proposals. Vince Cable, the government's Business Secretary, recently announced plans to have binding votes on directors' pay plans every three years.

[46] Ariely, Dan, *The Upside of Irrationality: The Unexpected Benefits of Defying Logic at Work and at Home* (HarperCollins 2010).

While they worked hard, diligently, and successfully when offered modest incentives, the rats choked under the pressure of stretching for a big prize. Immediately the cynic would be thinking, 'Yeah sure, fascinating stuff. Rats eh? How very relevant'. But obviously Ariely is well versed at dealing with cynics and, therefore, moved onto testing in humans. I assume it was to his great pleasure that he found exactly the same reaction, with humans choking under the pressure of outsized compensation.

Of course, no executive management team (or portfolio manager) would ever admit that the size of their bonus could in any way damage or adversely affect their behaviour. Any reasonable chief executive would claim it ludicrous to believe he might massively gear up a company's balance sheet if his bonus was linked to return on equity, or freeze capital expenditure if cash flow was important, or even constantly talk up his company's prospects if total shareholder return was of the utmost importance. Well, he might claim it was ludicrous, but did the incentivisation schemes from which banks' management benefited really assist them in making the best decisions?

We have also noticed Remuneration Committees react when operating conditions, say general economic weakness, are such that bonus targets will not be met. This, we are told, is just shockingly bad luck and runs the risk of leaving the management team under-remunerated through no fault of their own.

The solution? Easy. Rewrite the schemes. I do have some sympathy for this. Bad luck is no-one's fault and perhaps should be allowed for. But to keep it symmetrical, shouldn't we also adjust for good luck, such as excellent trading conditions, low raw material costs, and so on? We are still awaiting refunds from management who felt their rewards were the result of luck rather than skill.

My marketing team always requests that I sign off with a pithy comment that explains the relevance of my commentary to the day-to-day running of a fund. Unfortunately, there's no easy win here.

As part owners of the companies in which we invest, we have a duty to ensure that management are acting in the best interests of long-term shareholders. Outsized rewards, for both success and failure, do nothing to align management with shareholders, nor create the best environment for management to make the correct long-term decisions for their companies. We anticipate greater debate on this subject.

November 2010

Cost-cutting – too good to be true?

Gareth Jenkins recently retired from his position as Chief Executive of Imperial Tobacco Group, a position he held for 14 years. In that time, Mr Jenkins made some very successful acquisitions and it is widely accepted that he ran the company very efficiently. Following his retirement, his trusty lieutenant Alison Cooper has taken the reins. Analysts are, rather ironically given their great respect for her predecessor, feverishly anticipating her strategic moves, with many in particular expecting a new raft of cost-cutting.

Shareholders and analysts typically applaud cost-cutting; providing the cuts are not competed away, it is a simple way to increase profitability. But is such confidence in the virtues of cost-cutting always justified? Virtually all corporate management teams are incentivised on some combination of targets on profitability, cash

> "As outsiders, can we differentiate between good cost-cutting and bad cost-cutting?"

flow and share price performance (which is itself usually determined by the first two factors). Profit growth can be achieved through growing revenues, but cost-cutting is just as effective. Reducing advertising, using cheaper materials, taking health and safety a little less seriously, or pushing suppliers for lower prices will all impact positively in the short term and may even prove longer lasting. It is only when events turn sour (BP, Northern Rock, for example) that it becomes clear that management had long finished cutting flesh and had been working into the bone.

As outsiders, can we differentiate between good cost-cutting and bad cost-cutting? For example, a reduction in a company's advertising budget may initially be interpreted negatively. But it could be an indicator of improved value in advertising, through reduced rates, a greater share of voice (i.e. gaining advertising share over competitors), or better negotiation of advertising rates. These possibilities would change the negative to a positive and thoughtful investor relations would ensure the market's understanding.

This suggests two areas for investigation. If the profit margin of a company is very high relative to competition, then it is as well to be concerned as impressed. Although the company may offer several plausible reasons for superior performance, its prices may simply be too high or its costs too low. Secondly, as the cycle of permanent cost-cutting is stretched, the greater the chance that essential costs are removed.

It is not difficult to see why many companies' margins are cyclical: at an underperforming company, new management acts to increase operating margins until eventually they are raised to unsustainable levels. A combination of managerial arrogance and overconfidence as well as competitor catch-up subsequently sucks them back into the pack. (This suggests that a company with an average operating margin and return on capital may be a better company than it appears, as it invests for the longer term rather than to beat short-term targets.)

This margin cycle theory can be extended from one company to the market. Costs can be cut in all companies: staff encouraged to work harder or cut corners, customers forced to queue for longer, machines run into the ground or depreciated over a longer time, and suppliers asked to price more cheaply. In the short to medium term, margins can rise inexorably. Perhaps overall it is, therefore, not a great surprise that the assumption for operating margins in many Western markets is that they return to their all-time highs. This suggests a massive transference of value from employees (and suppliers in particular) to employers (aka companies). History, however, informs us that profit margins, particularly at an aggregate level, are mean reverting and we see little reason why this relationship should no longer stand. The drivers may not be obvious, but that does not make the conclusion any less likely.

How can we build the cyclicality of margins into our investment process? We prefer to participate nearer the start of the margin improvement stories, as we find these more reliable and less risky than supporting sustained improvement. However, this is far from straightforward as it is often tricky for an outsider to determine if a company is run inefficiently. There may be no direct competitors to benchmark margins against, or management may have spun a story of structurally higher costs raising low margins. Despite this caveat, a bet on reversion to the mean remains superior to one betting on trees growing to the sky.

July 2010

5.

Chancellor for a Day

The Perils of Economic Forecasting

Chancellor for a day

Many years ago as an A-Level Economics student, I participated in a group competition with my fellow spot-ridden and unenthusiastic peers. We were provided with a computer model of the UK economy that allowed manipulation of short-term interest rates and tax rates, and were challenged to generate as much economic growth as possible within a targeted inflation range.

With the innocence of youth, and the self-confidence of an average Chancellor of the Exchequer, we went to work. After just one or two small adjustments to the variables under our control, we had soon created one or two minor economic problems and, by the time the two-hour session was over, we had virtually bankrupted the UK economy.

With hindsight we were years ahead of our time. Much has been written by City commentators on quantitative easing (QE). Discussions have centred on its meaning, its purpose, and its consequences. However, when reading these documents, I have flashbacks to my own little experiment in economic management and the unintended consequences that flowed from our fairly small moves. The only sensible conclusion I can reach is that it is impossible to tell whether QE (and any sons and daughters of QE) will have the intended consequence of increasing bank lending, but it is far more likely that it will create a number of unintended consequences. And it is even more likely that irrespective of the final outcome, it will create **fear** of a number of unintended consequences.

So what should we worry about? Most lists would probably include inflation, deflation, financial instability, social unrest, recession, and depression (and for the real pessimists, war). We are using two asset classes to protect us from the whole gamut of nastiness: gold shares and index-linked gilts. Obviously, we cannot guarantee they will work, but at least we are trying.

"It is impossible to tell whether QE will have the intended consequence of increasing bank lending"

A client recently told me that when he started work as a private client fund manager in 1980, all his employer's private clients had between 1% and 2% of their portfolios invested in gold. This was apparently the norm in the industry, with the fund managers busy fighting the soon-to-be-ended battle against inflation. Given the finite supply of gold, any similar approach by fund managers now would probably be very positive for the gold price.

Perhaps the time to reduce our exposure to gold will therefore be when we are no longer asked to justify its position in our portfolios?

February 2009

Economic forecasting I – what's the point?

A question we are commonly asked when marketing is: 'Why do you not use a view on major economic statistics to shape your portfolio?' Sometimes it is a touch more incredulous: 'How on earth can you manage a fund without an economic view?' Perhaps we should consider it a compliment that these people believe we have a vision of the future that is worth inflicting on them and their clients. As much as I hate to disappoint them, we have no such vision. The reason for this is clear. We have no competitive advantage in this area and without a competitive advantage one is destined to underperform. (Incidentally, we are not alone here. Although I have never carried out a survey, I would guess the list of those economists with great forecasting track records is depressingly short.)

Let's imagine that we did have the skills necessary to provide accurate economic forecasts. How would we use the results? Conventional wisdom states that under certain economic conditions some events are highly probable and therefore it is reasonably obvious which shares to purchase to benefit from, say, increasing inflation, lower gross domestic product growth, or weak sterling. Except when it

> "Without a competitive advantage one is destined to underperform"

isn't. I stumbled across a nice example of this only the other day when an investment bank's report on the UK real estate sector highlighted that 'real estate and sterling tend to move together (1997-2007 was the exception to the rule)'. So other than a 10-year period in a graph covering a span of 32 years, this 'strong' relationship could be trusted.

"You're terrible at numeracy and economics – you could be an ideal future Chancellor of the Exchequer."

Having no view on future economic outcomes is different to denying that alternative economic outcomes will create varied conditions for the companies in which we invest. Of course they will and we can use this to our advantage. If other investors are terribly bearish about, say, the UK economy, they may sell certain shares at virtually any price. If this selling gathers pace, the share price may eventually discount a deep recession (or worse). If we bide our time, we will receive a 'cheap bet' on the future. For example, when we purchased our final tranche of Travis Perkins shares in late 2008 the shares were discounting a level of earnings way below anything the company had generated in the previous decade, and one which we thought was only possible if economic Armageddon occurred.

However, the Travis Perkins example was in all likelihood an extreme event. More probable is that a share falls because investors fear a dreaded profits warning will accompany deteriorating trading conditions. While we realise that short-term investors are obsessed with forecasting short-term events, this does not need to shape our behaviour. We are fixated on what normalised profits a company can generate, not what they will achieve in the next three months. Obviously if there is a recession, these normalised profits will arise later than might be ideal, but that is fine if the shares have been purchased sufficiently cheaply.

Benjamin Graham, the founding father of value investing, coined the term 'margin of safety' in the 1930s to explain this point. One way to think about this concept is that the difference (or margin) between fair value and current value is the value of the mistakes we can make before permanently losing money on a purchase. This allows for specific mistakes, oversights, accounting nasties, or shocking economic conditions. Fortunately, at purchase it is not necessary to articulate how we intend to use the margin of safety. We believe the important factors are that it is sufficiently large and that the value of the 'mistakes' that could materialise are reasonably limited.

Despite our spirited defence of forecasting futility, the cynics always feel they hold the knock-out punch by drawing attention to the gold shares in our portfolio, as this apparently 'proves' we take at least a passing interest in economic outcomes. That passing interest reveals we are in the middle of a huge financial experiment conducted by many of those who have created today's uncomfortable situation. A cursory thought is sufficient to appreciate that it could well end in disaster and, therefore, we believe an insurance policy in the shape of gold shares is a useful part of the portfolio. We would compare this to buying building insurance on our houses despite having no view on the likelihood of them burning down.

April 2010

Economic forecasting II – sure thing?

I recently stumbled across a reference to a lecture made by the famous economist John Maynard Keynes entitled 'Some Economic Consequences of a Declining Population'.[47] The lecture began:

> We know much more securely than we know almost any other social or economic factor relating to the future, that, in the place of the steady and indeed steeply rising level of population which we have experienced for a great number of decades, we should be faced in a very short time with a stationary or a declining level.

Keynes was apparently part of the consensus with this view: the Government Actuary was forecasting a population for Britain of just 34 million people by the year 2000.

This made me wonder if there are any current forecasts offered as a sure thing rather than representing a

"There is something to be said for siding with the consensus"

rough estimate of the future. Straight in at number two is climate change, with analysts eager to out-extrapolate each other to produce the scariest long-term vision of the future. While there are non-believers, the majority of them are regarded as denialists, so commentary arguably remains quite one-sided. But, rather like Pascal's Wager (he suggested betting on the existence of God because there was little downside but good upside to the wager) on balance there is something to be said for siding with the consensus.

---

[47] Some Economic Consequences of a Declining Population, The Galton Lecture, Eugenics Review vol xxix, no 1, 1937, referenced in *The Pinch* by David Willetts (Atlantic Books, 2010).

However, way, way ahead in first place is the conventional wisdom that emerging market economies will generate strong economic growth over the next few decades. Maybe they will, but I am fascinated by how little discussion there is on the claim. Given the near 100% error made by Keynes *et al.* in population forecasting, this suggests investors should ensure they secure attractive odds on even the most likely winning bets.

July 2010

Deeply double dippy

I have absolutely nothing of value to add on the economic outlook and spend what many regard as a comically small amount of time (let's round it down to zero) worrying about such matters. However, on my way to the sports pages each morning, I must admit to a brief sortie to the financial news. One does not need to skim-read for too long before a talking head claims that the 'likelihood of a double-dip recession is now much lower' or 'the risk of a double-dip recession has now passed'.

These claims interest me. They are based on the release of 'improved' economic data and while intuitively they make sense, scratch the surface and

> "Double dips can only be spotted with hindsight"

they become rather more questionable. After all, the levels of certain indicators (e.g. surveys of consumer confidence) were so low they could virtually fall no further, while other data such as economic growth were unlikely to keep falling at the same rate (or else there would be almost no economy left to measure). So 'improved' should really be replaced with 'less bad'.

However, let's just assume that economic data is improving. Does that really prove that the risks of a double dip are diminished? For that to be the case we would need to know what evidence the double-dip non-believers would require to lose their confidence. After all, better economic data would support their position while deteriorating data would be a worsening recession. The only circumstance left to dent their beliefs is therefore a double dip itself, by which time it is too late to react!

I therefore conclude that double dips can only be spotted with hindsight, as the first part of a double dip is identical to an economic recovery. Therefore, they strike me as being of more interest to historians than investors.

Perhaps quite a nice example of this can be found on a great website: **www.newsfrom1930.blogspot.com**. On this site an enthusiast, who has diligently worked his way through the *Wall Street Journal* archives of the 1930s, highlights the improving sentiment of commentators and investors, positive reading of economic data, and miscellaneous bullish stories. One example of such excessive optimism from the past is:

> There's a large amount of money on sidelines waiting for investment opportunities; this should be felt in market when "cheerful sentiment is more firmly entrenched". Economists point out that banks and insurance companies "never before had so much money lying idle".

Despite this reasonably widely held belief that the worst was over, US equities subsequently fell another 33%!

August 2009

6.

A Night on the Town

'Out with the Crowd' on Behavioural Finance

Behavioural finance – a night on the town

Keen to show that we are rounded people with active social lives and not just work nerds, a few colleagues and I shared an evening out last month. Eager to see the hottest show in town, we trotted down to the Adelphi Theatre in the West End of London to see Derren Brown. Mr Brown is a wonderful performer who, on his own website, describes his craft as "a mixture of magic, suggestion, psychology, misdirection and showmanship". The show ended in rapturous applause and the audience left on a high, generally amazed at the experience. Everyone was taken by different parts of the show and most had their views on how the 'tricks' had been conducted.

Once the magic of the night had worn off, I started thinking less about Mr Brown and more about his assistants. Generally, they were selected from the audience in a fairly arbitrary way, but, at certain points in the show, it was clear Mr Brown was more concerned with attracting the right sort of helper. At the beginning of the second half of the performance we were encouraged to close our eyes and fall into a deep sleep, assisted by the soothing words of our MC. Believe me I tried, as did my colleagues and my sister (who rarely stops talking long enough to draw breath), but nothing we heard or experienced could knock us from our (fairly) normal state of mind.

When we looked around to see who had slipped into a trance, I was surprised that the victims really seemed to be 'gone'. Their heads were lolling about and their bodies were relaxed. Cynically, I had thought that the most affected people would be those most eager to go on stage, but their trance-like states appeared to be genuine.

Most of the audience walks into the theatre just to see Mr Brown at work. However, for some of his tricks he requires a particularly suggestible type of person. The trance experiment is designed to pinpoint these people and Mr Brown can be confident they will behave in a predictable manner once in this state.

115

Why is this relevant to a monthly investment commentary? I believe "suggestibility" rears its ugly head in a number of different environments and particularly the stock market. Wikipedia informs me that according to Wagstaff (1991), attempts to isolate a global trait of "suggestibility" have been unsuccessful, due to an inability of the available testing procedures to distinguish measurable differences between the following distinct types of "suggestibility":

i. To be affected by a communication or expectation such that certain responses are overtly enacted, or subjectively experienced, without volition, as in automatism.

ii. Deliberately to use one's imagination or employ strategies to bring about effects (even if interpreted, eventually, as involuntary) in response to a communication or expectation.

iii. To accept what people say consciously, but uncritically, and to believe or privately accept what is said.

iv. To conform overtly to expectations or the views of others, without the appropriate private acceptance or experience; that is, to exhibit behavioural compliance without private acceptance or belief.

Although much of that may read like psycho-babble, the gist is that suggestible people are prone to uncritically accept what they are told and to act on it whether they believe it or not.

"Some people are hard-wired to be cynical rather than suggestible"

One of the classic suggestibility periods in recent times probably occurred when investors happily accepted the tenuous arguments made for buying technology stocks and then, despite the extraordinary valuations, purchased them anyway! The dreams and stories peddled endlessly in equity markets by company management, stockbrokers, and corporate financiers implies that suggestible people should run a mile from stock markets, but the continuing occurrence of asset bubbles tells us they do the opposite. However, we do know, almost by definition, that bubbles create the conditions that maximise the number of suggestible people in a group, so perhaps we should not be too hard on the bubbleistas.

So how can we avoid suffering from suggestibility? It is possible that some people are hard-wired to be cynical rather than suggestible. If that is true, it would certainly be a pleasant genetic head start. On the other hand, given how dangerous the results of suggestibility can be, perhaps we should empower ourselves to actively fight it by, for example, fixating on the risks of investing rather than the rewards. As legendary investor Seth Klarman puts it, "If you get the risk right, returns will come".

July 2009

"We're not sure if he's tired,
hungover, or still in a trance from
last night's Derren Brown show."

Framing – the benefit of the doubt?

It is perhaps alarming that with my appalling A-level results[48] I found gainful employment in the City. I definitely benefited from the 'framing effect' in the recruitment process. Our good friends at Wikipedia inform me that framing "describes that presenting the same option in different formats can alter people's decisions". I achieved a grade A in my Maths A-level, an odd bedfellow to my O grade in Further Maths. On its own, my poor grade in Further Maths marked me down as a pretty mediocre mathematician. However, placed alongside my Maths A-level, the grades suggested something deeper was at work – an off day perhaps, or illness? Despite my best, and rather naive, attempts to argue against this, it was clear that I often received the benefit of the doubt. And the more I disputed it, the more humble I was considered, thus further aiding my employment prospects.

Framing is all around us. Taking a dislike to a person on a first meeting (perhaps because they were late) often requires a great deal of disconfirming evidence to reverse the decision. However, if the same person's first dose of lateness is well into a successful relationship, it is more likely to be overlooked.

Similarly, it is easy to be turned off a stock if a negative thought arises early in the analysis, but which might have been viewed with indifference if it had only been uncovered after a 'buy' decision had been made.

We try to overcome framing – and a host of other behavioural biases – by remaining as objective as possible throughout the analytical process. This necessitates assessing all the positives and negatives completely, before reaching a conclusion. While this may sound straightforward, it is much harder to implement successfully. Knowing our weakness is merely the start of the journey.

November 2009

---

[48] See 'Expertise – keep practising' (page 34).

Nostalgia bias – nostalgia's not what it used to be

As Andy Murray missed his big chance at the Australian Open Tennis final, his mum possibly consoled herself with thoughts that at least his excellent showing in the tournament may have put him in the frame for the BBC Sports Personality of the Year Award. History suggests she should not get too excited, as sporting success early in the year tends to receive far less attention than similar success achieved closer to voting time. After all, despite Phil 'The Power' Taylor dominating the 'sport' of darts for the last 15 years, a period when he failed to win the World Championships only twice, he has yet to be crowned the people's favourite.[49] Perhaps the British public are simply anti-darts and I am underestimating Mr Murray's chances.[50] It is more likely, though, that the voters are suffering from 'recency bias' and by polling time have all but forgotten 'The Power's' earlier successes. Behavioural psychologists use 'recency bias' to explain how our behaviour is affected more by our most recent memories than by more relevant, but less recent occurrences.

Recency bias occurs everywhere. One classic example is to call the key witness last in a court case to leave the greatest possible impression on the jury. Many examples exist in the stock market too. For example, analysts often illustrate the cheapness of a stock by highlighting that its rating is as low as it has been for 10 years, but fail to explain why any periods previous to that are irrelevant.

But is it also possible to suffer from 'nostalgia bias'? Despite my best efforts I can find no academic evidence to support this, but it seems logical that we get nice warm feelings about events that happened long ago. For example, we all know that in the good old

---

[49] He (eventually) achieved 2nd place in December 2010.

[50] In July 2012 Andy Murray became the first Brit to reach the men's singles final at Wimbledon since 1938. In the year of the London Olympics even this achievement may prove insufficient for him to be made BBC Sports Personality of the Year.

days Curly Wurlys[51] were longer, footballers were more skilful, and sitcoms were funnier. Except that a lot of the time, they weren't. It's just that the constant reminiscing about them, and the happy memories of events that accompanied them, cloud our judgement.

It strikes me that investors are sensitive to nostalgia bias. A stock that has proved to be profitable in the past is considered more likely to generate profits in the future. This can quickly lead to overconfidence ('I know this stock really well. I have traded it profitably a number of times') and the embarrassment that often follows. A recent example of this is in the banking sector. Many US investors profited from the sector's difficulties during the Savings and Loan Crisis in the 1980s and thought they noticed similar characteristics when the most recent banking crisis began. Quite logically, they believed that the balance sheets of banks could weather the storm and that their high levels of operating profits would eventually recover any losses. Their nostalgia bias hampered any rational thoughts about the differences between the two crises, and great losses were consequently incurred.

The comforting news is that Warren Buffett appears to suffer from nostalgia bias too, albeit in a non-costly way. Alice Schroeder, biographer of

"Investors are sensitive to nostalgia bias"

Warren Buffett, has highlighted how Berkshire Hathaway's deal to buy Burlington Northern Santa Fe isn't the first time Buffett has invested in one of his lifelong interests. His first childhood business was selling chewing gum, and he put money into Wrigley last year. His second was selling Coca-Cola, and Berkshire Hathaway owns 200 million shares in the company today. Buffett's relationship with the bank Goldman Sachs, another of his investments, began when his father took him on a trip to New York City to meet the firm's chairman on his tenth birthday. It is clear, however, that while

---

[51] See also 'The risks of structural decline – a requiem to fondue sets' (page 11).

Buffett may feel comfortable with brands he knows well, he reduces the risk of bias with extraordinary amounts of patience, sometimes dealing many years after his initial interest in a company.

So how can we protect ourselves from these biases? Cures are too much to hope for but, as always, an admission that the risk exists at least alerts us to potential pitfalls. One approach we use is to study a company's history in great detail when we are analysing it. (Strangely enough, most investors spend the majority of their time 'analysing' the future, but we often remind ourselves that this is simply guessing under a fancier name.) With substantial data available we are more likely to appreciate the ebbs and flows of business cycles and not extrapolate short-term movements as deep-seated trends. Similarly, it may be more beneficial reading analysis which is, say, two years old, in preference to a recently published two page note on a company's results.

January 2010

How many spectators does it take to trigger a Mexican Wave?

When market volatility is very high, our marketing department usually rushes over to request a 'thought piece' that peers through market uncertainty and investor unease and makes sense of the general confusion. The request is really threefold: explain why the markets have sold off, rationalise the reasons, and end with a suitably bullish comment.

The first part is pretty straightforward. Nothing usually 'happens' to tip the market over the edge (the old adage about the presence of more sellers than buyers may be curt and unhelpful, but is often reasonably accurate). Sometimes information that was available in the days, weeks, or months before is suddenly interpreted differently and becomes a focal point for concern. While it would be ideal to have precise reasons for events, life is not that easy. I can still find no reason why the tech bubble burst when it did.

Fortunately, my twelve year old son shed some light on the subject. One of his favourite television programmes is *Brainiac*, which he assures me is a fun, yet educational, science programme. One of the experiments they constructed was to study how many football spectators were required to trigger a Mexican Wave. The scientists started with one spectator (the poor chap looked pretty stupid having to sit down after failing miserably) and continued adding one more until the Wave successfully worked its way around the whole ground. The magic number is clearly meaningless, but my son tells me it was seven spectators.

> "I can still find no reason why the tech bubble burst when it did"

Six spectators produced nothing. Zippo. Nada. Seven spectators had virtually the whole crowd on their feet. I would suggest that all that has changed in financial market this summer is that six has gone to seven.

Of course, the experiment was not entirely foolproof, as I daresay seven people attempting to trigger a Mexican Wave in the San Siro stadium (capacity approximately 85,000) might struggle, but would have a good chance of success at Victoria Road, home of Dagenham and Redbridge FC (capacity of 6,078). I think there may be a parallel in financial markets. If markets are very cheap and discounting a very low level of profits, a bear market is hard to trigger, but if markets are extended, full of bulls, and discounting a high level of profits, a fall is more likely to be sustained.

Is volatility good or bad? Well it's bad if you are a private client stockbroker and have a selection of neurotic clients giving you the 'screaming abdabs'[52] when markets are lurching around. If, on the other hand, you are a contrarian investor who feeds off those occasions when investors are at their most irrationally pessimistic, then volatility is undeniably positive and provides more opportunities to purchase stocks at larger than average discounts to their intrinsic value. This statement is not quite as suitably bullish as the marketers would wish, but our emphasis on stocks in preference to markets precludes any grander statements.

August 2011

---

[52] An attack of extreme anxiety or frustration. An expression often used by my dad when half-wits are driving him mad.

Being Wrong – did I really say that?

A new book by Kathryn Schulz, *Being Wrong: Adventures in the Margin of Error*,[53] is a fascinating study of errors. This is a great subject for any investor to ponder as we all make so many of them. Fortunately, we get the opportunity to learn from our errors and change our behaviour instead of finding ourselves in front of employment tribunals at the first sign of trouble. However, the luxury of assessing one's errors is often offset by the belief that we were not actually wrong. Rather than writing a book review, never one of my strengths, I have highlighted a few areas that caught my interest. Some of the book's ideas were new to me, some were reminders of classic studies: all of them made me consider the positives and pitfalls of contrarian investing.

> "The luxury of assessing one's errors is often offset by the belief that we were not actually wrong"

Ebbinghaus's Curve of Forgetting

My parents' generation are certain they remember where they were when they heard John Fitzgerald Kennedy had been shot. I am not sure what the equivalent is for my generation. For years, I remembered vividly the death of Elvis Presley, mainly because it coincided with a family holiday and an England versus Australia Test Match. I was positive for a long time afterwards that the opera star Maria Callas died on the same day, only to discover she actually died a month later. Ebbinghaus devised a curve of forgetting, and

---

[53] Schulz, Kathryn, *Being Wrong: Adventures in the Margin of Error* (Ecco Press, 2010).

other researchers added to his work to prove that the importance of an event has no bearing on how quickly we forget the details. Not only do our parents not always correctly remember where they were when Kennedy was shot, they also subsequently forget many other details of that momentous event at the same rate as information about the day before Kennedy was shot.

Connected to this are various studies of the reliability of eyewitness statements. The conclusion Schulz makes is that these statements can be shockingly unreliable. This is a slight problem for a defendant, as juries consider witness statements far more important than anything else available as evidence (other than DNA, I suppose) in a court of law.

Hamlet: Man or Mouse?

Schulz also highlights uncertainty and, in particular, the feelings of others towards it. She explains that in Shakespeare's *Hamlet*, the main character is visited by the ghost of his murdered father, who instructs him to slay his murderer. To make this a tad more complicated, Hamlet's father, the King of Denmark, has been murdered by his brother, who has gone on to marry Hamlet's mother. So Hamlet is being asked to murder his stepdad, his uncle, and his King. The modern view of Hamlet is that, although it is a ghost entreating him to carry out revenge, he does a great deal of dithering before making his decision and therefore is a bit of a weak bloke. (Interestingly, the first 150 years after Shakespeare wrote the play, Schulz reports that Hamlet was held in far greater esteem – "vigorous, bold and heroic".)

Uncertainty in people is typically an undesirable trait, particularly in those who have been appointed as decision makers: monarchs, politicians, even fund managers. Certainty in one's views is sought by others, whereas floundering and indecisiveness – even if it reflects a careful assessment of a massive amount of conflicting data – is seen as inappropriate. When discussing certainty, Schulz quotes

Rollo May, a psychologist, as saying that our commitment to an idea "is healthiest when it is not without doubt, but in spite of doubt".

Solomon Asch

Schulz also details a classic psychology test involving one volunteer and an army of stooges, repeated a number of times with only the volunteer changing. These people are all asked to look at a card on which there is a single line and are simultaneously shown another card on which there are three lines marked A, B, and C. They are then asked whether line A, B, or C is identical to the single line on the first card. It is not a trick question. In fact, it is harder to imagine an easier multiple-choice question.

This exercise was conducted in two ways: one in private and one where everyone shouted out their answer in turn, the volunteer last. In private, the success rate for the volunteers was virtually 100%. However, under open outcry with the stooges intentionally providing the incorrect answer, the success rate of the volunteers plummeted to 63%.

For many years it was thought that it was the stooges' mob effect that made the volunteers call out obviously incorrect answers. However, when this experiment was repeated decades later, the volunteers' brains were monitored and an even stranger effect of the stooges was detected: they actually affected the volunteers' judgement of the length of the line.

Groupthink

Irving Janis conducted much of the original work on groupthink in the late 1960s. He defined it as: "A mode of thinking that people engage in when they are deeply involved in a cohesive in-group, when the members' strivings for unanimity override their motivation to realistically appraise alternative courses of action," and held it responsible for several poor political decisions in the 1960s. He believed groupthink particularly affected homogeneous, close-knit communities overly insulated from internal and external criticism and who felt under pressure from outsiders. He claimed these groups were noticeable for their tendencies to censor dissent, reject criticisms, and operate with a conviction of moral superiority.

Schulz highlights that Janis's analysis suggested groupthink drove major decisions during episodes in the Bay of Pigs Invasion and the Vietnam War. In general, Janis believed groupthink was caused by members of a group wishing to avoid embarrassing or angering other members, or by a desire to avoid looking foolish. In his book, *Groupthink*, Janis lists a number of ways of avoiding the curse of groupthink:

> i) At least one group member should be assigned the role of Devil's Advocate
> ii) Outside experts should be invited into meetings
> iii) All effective alternatives should be examined

and, one which Schulz omits:

> iv) Senior ranks should not express an opinion when assigning a task to a group

Identifying Mistakes

Professor Philip Tetlock, a psychologist and political historian, specialises in tracking the judgements of 'experts' (Schulz does not cover this, but Tetlock discovered over a 20 year study that experts' predictions of the future are only slightly more accurate than chance). Tetlock's efforts to understand the source of experts' errors was greatly frustrated because the experts claimed they had given answers far more accurate than those recorded.

Schulz later details an amusing number of 'wrong buts' that are often used by people making mistakes in a blatant effort to minimise their responsibilities. (It struck me that these are possibly the excuses that give gamblers the stamina to persevere):

I was wrong but I will be right next year

I was wrong but it wasn't my fault

I was wrong but there was a 'left-field' event that ruined everything

I was wrong but I was very close to being right

I was wrong but my choice was by far the most sensible

Conclusion

How does an excellent book such as *Being Wrong* tie into and assist with asset management? Typically, investors are encouraged to have well-defined investment processes, but the stricter the process and the greater the similarity of a team's investors, the greater the risk of groupthink. We must always discipline ourselves to analyse arguments in several ways, even if we risk appearing less certain than our peers. But I am sure all teams remain vulnerable to the curse of groupthink. Similarly, as much as we know our thinking must not be affected by mob rule, it is easier to be aware of the affliction than to correct it.

And finally, three times this year I have been guilty of buying a stock and then, after further thought, selling it not long after. Perhaps rather than worrying that I am giving a good impression of cluelessness, I should be comforted that I am exhibiting my true dithering abilities.

September 2010

Overconfidence? No, I'm just right, I'm sure

Overconfidence is one of the many behavioural biases suffered by humans. This is consistently illustrated in surveys showing that a large majority of us believe we are better-than-average drivers, lovers, and sportspeople. Obviously, it is a mathematical truism that the majority cannot be better than average. Happily, once aware of this weakness, we can use this knowledge to improve our performance by, for example, driving at a slower speed. But what alterations can we make in the investment world to avoid this malady?

"I call this need to appear knowledgeable on all things 'The Black Cab Driver Syndrome'" I came across an academic paper this month, 'Managing Overconfidence' by Russo and Schoemaker,[54] which made some suggestions. First, the authors explain that because we are deficient in understanding the limits of our knowledge, we are always vulnerable to overconfidence. Perhaps fund managers particularly suffer because they are constantly encouraged to provide their views on an array of subjects at conferences and seminars and virtually derided if they answer: 'I don't know' or 'I don't really understand the issue well enough to have a sensible view'. I call this need to appear knowledgeable on all things 'The Black Cab Driver Syndrome'.

To develop a better understanding of how much we do and do not know, the authors suggest two key elements: feedback and accountability. Feedback on our performance could not be easier for

---

[54] Russo, J. Edward and Paul J.H. Schoemaker (1992), 'Managing Overconfidence', *Sloan Management Review*, 33, 7-17.

investors. Performance figures are very accessible and can be interrogated in detail to study the success or otherwise of individual decisions. And, if we have documented our reasons for making these decisions, accountability will be clear.

Russo and Schoemaker highlight the following common causes of overconfidence:

Availability: failing to consider all the potential scenarios.

Anchoring: focusing on one value or idea and not adjusting away from it sufficiently.

Confirmation bias: ignoring any disconfirming evidence.

Hindsight: making us believe the world is more predictable than it really is.

They also offer five techniques to overcome it:

i.   Accelerated feedback: how many previous decisions with this level of confidence were wrong? What mistakes were made?

ii. Counterargumentation: embrace the opposing views (or perhaps even better, do not reach a view too early).

iii. Paths to trouble: at its simplest, considering everything that could go wrong.

iv. Paths to the future: combining a number of the potential problems as well as the potential positives to create a range of scenarios (Charlie Munger refers to these combinations that create extreme outcomes as the "lollapalooza effect").

v.   Awareness of the problem: a catch-all to encompass any other techniques which the authors had not uncovered, but are used by those eager to control their overconfidence.

Can we suggest any non-Russo and Schoemaker techniques? First, by always committing to paper our reasons for purchasing stocks we keep track of our successes as well as our failures. This will highlight times when we were successful for the wrong reason and therefore hopefully prevent us from overstating our abilities. Second, we have strict rules on the amount we allocate to certain stocks or sectors, which allows for the fact that we may be wrong whatever the strength of our beliefs. Third, we wait for shares to significantly underperform before making our purchases, with the intention of creating a sizeable margin of safety to protect us from ignorance. Finally, we aim to act where we see the most attractive odds, i.e. where the market currently discounts the more bearish of the scenarios we have considered.

Of course, none of these techniques are perfect, but at least an awareness of our limitations provides some control over the nasty affliction of overconfidence.

October 2009

Availability bias – Thinking, Fast and Slow

One of the benefits of meeting clients is that they often provide insights about our competitors' current opinions. It is a particularly revealing exercise when we hear the same message repeatedly, as it suggests a consensus view has formed – an event that naturally raises our contrarian antennae.

A common argument we have heard is that despite concerns over patents, pricing, pipeline, and regulation, the much maligned pharmaceutical sector is attractive. Parallels with the tobacco sector of a decade or so ago apparently support this argument: despite its pariah status at the time, as a sector in structural decline and with ongoing legal expenses, tobacco stocks have performed phenomenally – up by over 1300% in total return terms since the end of 1999. So why, say these bulls, shouldn't pharmaceutical stocks pull off the same trick?

While considering this point I have been skipping through *Thinking, Fast and Slow* by Daniel Kahneman,[55] a psychologist who won the Nobel Prize in Economic Sciences in 2002 for the work he conducted with his academic partner Amos Tversky (who died in 1996) on uncertainty and decision making. The book is semi-auto-biographical and a great read. (As an aside, it is revealing that a significant percentage of the commonly used behavioural finance examples illustrating the irrationality of humans were the ideas of these two Israeli academics or their students.)

Two biases that Kahneman revisits from his work with Tversky, and which seem highly relevant to the tobacco versus pharmaceutical sector discussion, are those of availability and representativeness. A pinch of regret should also be added to this sordid emotional cocktail.

---

[55] Kahneman, Daniel, *Thinking, Fast and Slow* (Allen Lane, 2011).

The representativeness heuristic (rule-of-thumb strategy) encourages the brain to search for past events that are similar to the current experience. As a large defensive stock market sector, with earnings under pressure and several factors threatening its longer-term success, some investors are tempted to pair up the pharmaceutical sector with the tobacco sector of a decade ago.

The availability heuristic is a mental rule-of-thumb that uses the ease with which examples come to mind to make judgements about the probability of events. The regularity with which British American Tobacco (BAT) reaches all-time share price highs certainly makes it a very available example of how large blue chips are able to regain their mojo.

Regret is a tough emotion for us all to deal with: 'Why didn't I buy that stock/bet on that horse/use that great line?' type questions remind us that the future may have been significantly better if only we had taken a slightly different course. It must be galling for those technology investors, busy using price-to-eyeball ratios to assess the cheapness of stocks in the late 1990s, that a simple old-fashioned low price to earnings ratio would have uncovered far superior investments, such as the extraordinarily cheap tobacco stocks. It is too late to correct that oversight, but not too late to learn from it. And with tobacco stocks some of the biggest constituents of the FTSE 100 – BAT and Imperial Tobacco have a combined weighting of over 6% – regret just keeps prodding away.

Of course, over the years there have also been a number of stocks – the 'buggy whip manufacturers'[56] – that exhibited elements of structural decline and then proceeded to generate extraordinary underperformance. However, these stocks, as a result of their

---

[56] Thanks to a colleague for pointing me towards a YouTube clip from *Other People's Money* starring Danny DeVito (Warner Bros, 1991). In the clip, DeVito, a corporate raider, rails against the board of a sleepy manufacturing company reluctant to embrace technology and ridicules them for their strategy, which he believes is analogous to a desire to become the last buggy whip manufacturer.

appalling performance, are not high profile and therefore are more easily forgotten. Availability bias concentrates investors' minds on the easy to

"Regret is a tough emotion for us all to deal with"

remember winners, while representativeness bias is dangerous, as it encourages us to over-emphasise one or two reasonably small or irrelevant similarities and ignore the many falling knives that don't recover.

Certainly, tobacco companies have cut significant costs and the pharmaceutical companies may well copy, but the main driver for the extraordinary growth in profitability over the last decade has been tobacco price increases. Tobacco companies are fortunate to have customers who are addicted to their products and are, therefore, relatively price insensitive. It is unlikely that the pharmaceutical companies have similar pricing power, particularly as they are in the middle of a nasty multi-year period when a number of their drugs come off patent. To compound this, cash-strapped governments provide a large percentage of their revenues worldwide.

I am certainly not opposing the pharmaceutical sector bulls – we are overweight the sector ourselves – but find it difficult to see many parallels with the tobacco sector.

May 2012

Risk aversion – the attraction of the uninvestable

As an enthusiastic first year university student many years ago, I remember responding to my economics lecturer's recommendation and purchasing *Economics* by Professor Paul Samuelson.[57] I know my enthusiasm was short-lived as the book sits in immaculate condition on my shelves at home. Other than a spell working with Professor Samuelson's daughter a few years later, I confess I have spent little time thinking of him, or his work, in the intervening period. That has changed, as he received a few honourable mentions in the book I discussed last month, Daniel Kahneman's *Thinking, Fast and Slow*.

Kahneman relates that, in the early 1960s, Samuelson offered a friend a hypothetical gamble on a coin toss, in which heads would pay US$100, but tails would lose him $50. The friend rejected the bet, but offered to accept it if he could repeat it 100 times. Psychologists have apparently pored over this 'problem' for years to rationalise how a bet perceived as 'bad' can be considered 'good' if repeated often enough.

Samuelson's 'problem' explains many investors' actions: they are happy to hold a portfolio of stocks with the realisation that, although the pay-off of some individual stocks may be quite poor, in general the good and bad will approximately cancel out (and hopefully be slightly positive). In contrast, the risk of a very concentrated portfolio is that the chances of a really poor result are much greater – an unattractive bet for most professionals. However, investors appear to baulk at particular stocks. They are suddenly unable to consider a stock as part of a portfolio and instead regard it as a single

---

[57] Samuelson, Paul A., and William D. Nordhaus, *Economics: An Introductory Analysis* (McGraw-Hill, 1985).

bet. To justify their decision to avoid purchasing it, they typically announce that the stock is 'uninvestable' – a term designed to protect them from claims of incompetence in case the stock rises significantly.

BP is an interesting case study. After the disaster in the Gulf of Mexico, many investors gave the stock a wide berth, as they feared the company might be heavily fined or even face the prospect of bankruptcy. It is easy to understand their actions – when it is their job to convince themselves, their boss, and their clients that they have accurately modelled a company's prospects to the nth decimal place, it is difficult to allow for some large one-offs that may or may not occur. Even worse, to add to the feelings of repulsion, the risks of losing money heavily in a short time (due to, say, the size of the BP fine) were much higher. 'Death by a thousand cuts' often appears the more attractive way to lose clients' money, possibly because investors convince themselves they will have the good sense and timing to bail out a long time before losing all their stake.

While Kahneman and others have discussed Samuelson's 'problem' in terms of risk aversion (i.e. losses hurt people much more than similar sized gains), I believe it is a necessary consideration that many investors are concerned about the risk of sudden loss. As performance is judged over shorter and shorter time periods, actions that avoid or minimise the risks of downward lurches are increasingly attractive. Perhaps, if a potential investor in BP had been told that his performance would not be judged for, say, three years and even then would only be considered by analysing portfolio performance as a whole, the investor may have been a more willing buyer.

Although the BP situation was unique, there have been many parallels in stock market history. A number of companies have been found guilty of various misdemeanours (usually involving drugs, oil, or tobacco) and most recovered strongly from these events – in share price terms – within a few years. The tentative conclusion is that

"Many investors are concerned about the risk of sudden loss"

perhaps only ten or twenty of these 'disaster' occasions may arise over an investor's career, but the average pay-off from investing when investor sentiment has been very poor, has generally been very good (although admittedly with one or two blow-ups). That said, making a correct decision 'on average' is often identical to being wrong and may not be viewed sympathetically, particularly if the client has not benefited from good 'on average' decisions made years earlier.

Kahneman argues that sometimes it can be incorrect to make the single gamble even if it is mathematically attractive. Although he does not mention fund management specifically, he provides three conditions when it is a bad move: firstly, when such gambles are not independent (i.e. they are all reliant on the same event for a positive outcome); secondly, when the size of the bet can be bad for one's financial health if it goes wrong (i.e. it is too large a percentage of the portfolio); and thirdly, if the bet is very long odds. For example, making a series of bets at 100/1 because the correct odds are 50/1 is rationally correct, but it may take many years of bad results before success arrives.

June 2012

7.

Meet the Monkeys

Fund Management and Mismanagement

Star fund managers – meet the monkeys

One of the many positives often attributed to Sir Alex Ferguson, manager of Manchester United FC, is that he is an excellent seller of players. Football trivia kings can provide a seemingly endless list of players he bought who then raised their game at the Theatre of Dreams, but were subsequently shown the exit despite no obvious signs of deterioration in their skills. I am reasonably reliably informed that Messrs Hughes, Ince, Kanchelskis, Cole, Yorke, Van Nistelrooy, and Beckham all peaked during their time with Sir Alex.

Can we draw any conclusion other than the obvious from this 'study'? Love them or loathe them, there can be no dispute that Manchester United are quite a decent football team. Any centre forward joining them (even if he is from the local pub team) is likely to receive many more scoring opportunities than in his previous career and, therefore, appear more successful. However, on moving to a poorer club, his new colleagues are unlikely to make him look quite so talented.

Perhaps Manchester United's footballers can be compared with star fund managers? For both groups, it is not always easy to disaggregate the inherent ability of the individual and the environment in which they operate. A star fund manager (SFM) may appear to be a brilliant individual, but possibly a high percentage of his brilliance is due to a team of unsung analysts, the willingness of his boss to put up with any boorish behaviour during the good times while supporting him in tough times, and the ability of his salesmen to avoid performance-sapping redemptions at the bottom of the performance cycle. Softer factors such as an easy commute, a local sandwich shop, and friendly colleagues may also contribute to the package.

Remove a SFM from his environment and anything can happen. Of course, our marketing industry conveniently forgets this. There

"Remove a SFM from his environment and anything can happen" is, after all, a never-ending conveyor belt of potential SFMs ready to be promoted on the demise of others. But apparently investors like to buy into 'personalities'. Is this because it is easier to be convinced about the integrity, ability, judgement, or professionalism of a star individual as opposed to a more homogenous team of investment professionals? Or perhaps it is because when one thinks of a team, it is hard not to imagine the weaker players diluting the strong returns of the best players?

Maybe a SFM's behaviour changes as the marketing machine moves into full flow. Surely even SFMs have periods when they have fewer good ideas or even, God forbid, underperform. The pressurised performance-driven environment may not permit this and a SFM might start over-trading or drifting from his winning style in a desperate attempt to maintain a track record.

The 'hot hand' too should not be ignored when judging SFMs. Sportsmen often have runs of great form followed by runs of poor form. The important trade for them is to lock in long-term contracts and sponsorship deals at their peaks. A few good years of performance can bestow almost mystical powers on a SFM. However, it is humbling for us all to remember that providing you begin an exercise with a sufficiently large collection of dart-throwing monkeys one or two of them would rise to become SFMs. Provided their marketing departments could package them attractively ('Meet our Bottom Pickers'?) I assume the big fund flows would follow.

March 2010

Organogram chaos – specialists versus generalists

Clients who visit us to conduct due diligence on our funds often focus on the four P's – Philosophy, Process, People, and Performance. Unlike an exam, I work on the principle that there are no correct or incorrect answers – the clients are simply seeking to determine if the first three P's make sufficient sense to have accounted for historical performance and will combine to generate future performance. Is it a durable philosophy, implemented with a clear process by a talented, dedicated and stable team?

Most large-ish fund management groups run a variant of a fund manager/analyst model – a named fund manager supported by a team of analysts specialising in certain sectors and/or regions. This certainly looks very impressive on an organogram and the structure can be rationalised as one that utilises analysts' in-depth knowledge of individual companies and sectors.

Naturally, as contrarians, our approach is different. Although the traditional model is attractive for its logic and simplicity, we have always harboured concerns that it does not necessarily produce the best returns. Consider a sector that has been a poor performer for years. An analyst who had correctly identified the trend would probably hold entrenched views, little regard for management of companies within the sector and little belief that the trend would ever reverse. This lack of flexibility makes it very unlikely that he would identify the factors most relevant to change the sector's fortunes. In contrast, an analyst constantly bullish of a declining sector's prospects might be treated disdainfully by his colleagues and feel unable to capitulate on his sector stance as he would lock in a loss. It is difficult to believe his colleagues would still act on his 'buy' recommendation if it had repeatedly failed at higher prices.

"We're on our own now, Bongo ...
(sob) ... Bobo's run away to be a
fund manager!"

Another obstacle that sector specialists must overcome is the risk that industry 'expertise' accentuates the possibility of not seeing the wood for the trees. This can definitely arise in a sector with significant news flow. In this instance, an analyst is liable to delve too deeply into the minutiae to prove his knowledge and miss the changing trend.

There are also softer issues to consider – if the analyst has known management teams of companies in his sector and developed a close relationship over many years, he may be uncomfortable asking searching questions or he may even be simply bored or exhausted of looking at the same companies. (Somewhere in the distant past, I remember a colleague was desperate to cede analysis of the ever-falling housebuilding sector as he was psychologically exhausted by the waves of bad news and intermittent false dawns. We all laughed, but it was probably an excellent reason to grant his wish. Of course, the sector turned not long after.)

The risks are just as high for long-term analysts of successful companies. The analysts may be convinced, following a period of consistent and stable earnings growth, that these companies have powers allowing them to shrug off competition. This persuades them the shares should not be sold at any price. This can be a dangerous assumption, especially if both the rating of the shares and the profits of the company are high.

Finally, a sector analyst is very reluctant to confess to deficiencies in his knowledge. A bank analyst must have learnt and been surprised by much that has happened over the last five years (as is Bob Diamond apparently), but would still be expected by his colleagues to master endless acronyms, regulatory changes, and various other technicalities. Losing the option to throw one's hands in the air and exclaim that a sector is too complex to understand is a significant handicap.

An alternative to sector expertise is to employ generalists: analysts who will use their skills to study any company irrespective of its

"An alternative to sector expertise is to employ generalists"

sector. I dislike the term 'generalist' as it implies there is a lower knowledge base. That is probably true, but we believe the knowledge we forfeit is noise and babble. We are not participating in a pub quiz, merely trying to evaluate if a stock is cheap. Most stocks move over the long term for just one or two reasons and not because of the trivia.

The analysts can also approach each stock fresh and without any preconceptions. Why is the industry structured as it is? Could it change? Are the historical barriers to entry and other competitive advantages still pertinent? How can we oppose the conventional wisdom? Are the arguments bulls made to buy the shares at higher prices still relevant and, crucially, now accessible at a much lower valuation?

Our team is structured to create an investment process that we believe is most likely to create long-term performance rather than to ease box-ticking exercises for potential clients. We may consequently need to articulate our alternative approach, but we much prefer that than simply acting like the herd.

July 2012

Mis-selling – snake oil everywhere?

I love working in the fund management industry and am well aware that I could be less happily employed. Despite that, I don't find all that happens in our little world unremittingly positive. As an industry, we are often guilty of pushing ugly products down the throats of clients at unattractive times. Of course, it is not marketed like that. Instead investors are regaled with stories of diversification, high growth markets, and the promise of glorious returns. Most of this sales patter is supported by historical performance and obviously illustrates how much the client has already missed, but is designed to instil both fear and greed. There are very few occasions I can remember when fund management houses suggested it was a bad time to buy any of their funds.

Any investor receiving a smooth sales pitch should be highly cynical and search for the unspoken pitfalls or negatives in the investment case. This is far from easy for the general practitioner, particularly as there are few sources of truly independent research. How can one quickly oppose conventional wisdom on the attractive arguments of asset classes as diverse as, say, Chinese equities, timber, or German residential property?

There is no straightforward solution, although I will happily propose a few ideas. First, beware of anything that is selling successfully. As well as indicating a worrying popularity, it also highlights the story

> "Beware of anything that is selling successfully"

is well disseminated and implies the price of the asset probably reflects the potential good news. Examining unloved areas surely increases the chances of success. Secondly, emphasise the valuation rather than the story. Is the asset class cheap or does the buy argument centre on tucking this growth story away for the 'long term'? Paying up for dreams has rarely, if ever, proved worthwhile as long-term investors in technology funds know to their cost.

I am not suggesting that clients are lied to, just that they must be made aware that salesmen have significant biases. Even when the industry is in post-sales care and maintenance, the language remains at best baffling and at worst completely meaningless. For example, what does the phrase 'cautiously optimistic' mean? One can be cautious or optimistic but surely not both. 'Markets are likely to remain volatile' is typically paraded after a high level of volatility and is obviously incorrect as eventually volatility will fall. Meanwhile, 'the outlook is uncertain' suggests that most of the time it is very certain, a claim that is absurd.

My favourite (hated) lines begin 'with the benefit of hindsight' (a phrase virtually all MPs used to justify their behaviour once named and shamed for expense fiddling). Of course, we never have hindsight to guide our decisions, only a much tougher slice of foresight. Naturally, any MP warned that their claim would result in mass humiliation and possible court proceedings would never have acted in the way they did, and similarly, no investor would purchase a share they knew was going down. The pertinent question is whether they should have had the foresight to understand these risks.

I have often been marketed investments managed by a 'great team' or a 'strong board'. This is obviously nice to have, but harder to prove. Perhaps to be taken seriously, claims like this must be accompanied by an example of a bad team or a weak board that the salesman had previously promoted.

"Emphasise the valuation rather than the story"

Typically, it is sensible to run a mile if offered a product based on a computerised programme that 'back-tests well'. No rocket scientist would dream of selling a product that back-tests poorly. Data is mined comprehensively until a particularly impressive historical record is found. Consequently, a successful back-test is usually just a random sequence that often changes character soon after identification.

Of course, it is not possible to **make** money avoiding products (or people) with any of these warnings. Sometimes, however, it is as important to avoid making losses, and shunning snake oil salesmen and their terrible products can only be a positive in this regard.

June 2010

Marketing – weasel words I

There are some investment quotes that are imbued with knowledge and realism, but which to us make little sense. 'Poor earnings visibility' and 'dead money' are usually enough to make us splutter, but it is the mention of momentum that we find most troubling. Comments such as 'don't fight the current momentum' and 'in the short term, momentum is obviously with the shares' are typically sprinkled amongst financial reports and might convince the reader that a sensible point has been made.

The gist of such arguments is that investors would only wish to sell when the momentum driving a share price upwards has ended. Of course, this only becomes apparent when the price is falling. No other clues are provided. So these soothsayers are really saying 'stick with this share until it starts going down'. If it were that easy to play momentum, trouble-free profits would be available to all.

We are an industry of mouths on sticks and generally will provide an opinion on most subjects with little encouragement, regardless of whether we have anything sensible to add. The honest response when asked our view on the short-term performance of a share is, 'I don't know', but that does not typically generate fund inflows, confidence, or pay increases. And it is a particularly difficult response to give when momentum is 'obviously' with the shares, as one is vulnerable to the embarrassment of being wrong alone – a near unforgivable sin in investment markets.

Sometimes the herd will go against momentum, but in these circumstances language becomes far more negative with talk of 'spikes' and 'dead cat bounces'. To the agnostic of course, one man's spike is another man's momentum and the phrase chosen simply reflects whether a bull or bear is speaking. For example, in the market today, bears claim the 'dash for trash' should end soon, while the bulls argue that the cyclical rally is embryonic.

Of course, momentum is not necessarily bad for contrarian investors; it usefully provides liquidity when a share is pushed well beyond its fair value. Anti-momentum investors therefore enjoy the great luxury of having liquidity on their side, whereas it is the enemy of momentum investors. They must fight to participate in a story (and thus overpay) and then battle to exit a story (and thus accept a discounted price). This trading cost is generally ignored when discussing the merits of momentum-based strategies. While transparent dealing costs such as commission may have declined considerably in recent years, the hidden costs of dealing with the crowd have probably not.

Despite what we regard as many negatives (and although virtually all investors agree we should aim to buy low and sell higher, rather than buy high and hope some poor fool pays an even higher price), momentum investing remains a popular strategy.

> "Momentum is not necessarily bad for contrarian investors"

Perhaps its allure is because it appears to offer a sense of control ('sell when momentum goes') compared to the apparent risks of value investing ('sell when you can't take any more pain'). Whatever the reason, it is a strategy that is likely to continue to attract a strong following and an equally strong band of sceptics.

September 2009

Marketing – weasel words II

Over a month in which equity markets posted significant falls – and the falls continued into October – it was clear that investor sentiment had weakened considerably. Common quotes heard were: 'in these markets, capital preservation is key', 'I am happy to buy when there is less uncertainty', 'don't try to be a hero in these markets', and 'it's a sensible time to reduce risk'. These statements initially sound suitably prudent and logical, but I'm not convinced they are correct.

Studying each in turn:

'In these markets, capital preservation is key' – This presupposes that future market conditions will be as poor as recent market conditions and typically the high volatility and current uncertainty inform this view. It's curious that when markets hit all-time highs this quote is rarely heard.

'I am happy to buy when there is less uncertainty' – There are few things that can be guaranteed currently, but there can be no doubt that if the market moves lower there will be even greater uncertainty. Therefore, investors aiming to buy when there is less uncertainty wish to pay a higher price than is currently available. Is this sensible?

'Don't try to be a hero in these markets' – Well, when should one try to be a hero? When markets are hitting all-time highs, everyone is bullish, and risks seem non-existent? We believe more risk should be accepted if sufficient reward is offered as compensation. In our opinion, this usually occurs when volatility is high and investor sentiment poor.

'It's a sensible time to reduce risk' – A strategy of consistently reducing risk because of high volatility (i.e. after markets have fallen) is virtually certain to reduce long-term returns. It is best to make decisions on long-term risk management when conditions are stable.

October 2008

Surveys – 9 out of 10 Cats

I typically take survey findings with a very large pinch of salt. Many are conducted by pollsters with little interest in the subject and who are insufficiently motivated to secure a distribution of respondents that mirrors the underlying population. One must assume, for example, that a poll carried out by *The Jeremy Kyle Show*[58] at 9.30am on a weekday will not reflect the thoughts of a cross-section of the whole of British society. Investment surveys are often little better as the pollsters often seem to sit in a call centre randomly contacting anyone who works in asset management and with no interest in the precise role of any willing respondent.

With those caveats I less than enthusiastically read a recent survey, 'The Barings Investment Barometer', which purported to study the thoughts of 'investment professionals'. My cynicism was reinforced as I read the answer to one of the first questions: 'How well do you feel you know each of the following asset classes and sectors?' Intriguingly 6 of the 152 respondents answered that they were either 'quite unfamiliar' or 'very unfamiliar' with 'cash', which whatever way you cut it is rather worrying. However, the responses that really caught my attention were that 96% of investment professionals viewed emerging market equities favourably and 94% viewed Asian equities (excluding Japan) favourably. The commonality of opinions here is astonishing. We are, after all, dealing with the future – never easy to forecast at the best of times and particularly hard, I hear, to forecast at the moment. I would have assumed this would result in more varied opinions.

It is easy to imagine how these opinions are formed. The arguments for emerging market economies' superior prospects are

---

[58] Popular daytime British TV chat show. Members of the public try to resolve their family or personal problems while the host, Jeremy Kyle, acts as moderator-mentor. The live audience is also invited to participate in the discussion. The show often results in heated verbal exchanges and sometimes an attempted punch-up, typically following the outcome of a lie detector or paternity test.

widely understood, and naturally encourage respondents to prefer the equities of that region. You never know, they might even be correct. However, as I have mentioned before, one way of ensuring groupthink[59] doesn't take hold of a decision-making group is to appoint a Devil's Advocate. In the absence of anyone else, I will volunteer for this role.

True, much seems to strongly favour the emerging economies. But forecasting is rarely that straightforward. Wind the clock back about 25 years and I dare say the vibes on Japanese economic growth were similar. Emerging markets are still reliant on the developed economies for much of their growth, so perhaps this should concern the bulls. These economies are also very reliant on future Chinese growth. Such confidence is possibly justified, but it is interesting that so many capitalist investment professionals are certain a strongly communist controlled economy is assured of short-, medium- and long-term success.

Even if the economic bulls are correct, economic strength might not necessarily flow through to the stock market. The huge amount of capital individual companies have committed to the region could combine to damage overall returns. A shortage of labour in these thriving economies could force a transfer of value from companies to employees. And companies on high ratings might struggle to meet the lofty earnings expectations.

One question that particularly puzzles me is who on earth is selling these emerging market equities to allow the buyers to participate in this sure thing? What have they spotted to encourage them to bail out? Or have they discovered other asset classes that are even more attractive?

---

[59] See also 'Being Wrong – did I really say that?' (page 125).

One last thought. Even if it is correct to maximise one's exposure to these economies, a direct investment in the relevant equity markets may not be the most efficient strategy. Perhaps Unilever, HSBC, and a variety of Japanese exporters might offer both superior growth prospects and cheaper valuations? As a contrarian investor I can't help but be concerned by the strength of belief in emerging market equities. The lack of a balanced argument concerns me even more.

"Emerging markets are still reliant on the developed economies for much of their growth"

October 2010

8.

Colin the Contrarian

Tall Tales and Other Confessions

Colin the Contrarian – a cautionary tale

Colin the Contrarian had experienced a tough few years. He employed a falling knives investment strategy and in a spurt of professional diligence had even read some books on the subject. He knew there was danger in the strategy, so had followed a discipline of allowing these knives to fall significantly before he caught them. Patience was the key. Wait until the stocks represent option value and then swoop. Sure there would be some losers, but the spectacular winners would, history informed him, more than make up the difference.

However, despite applying great patience, he had suffered. First, the ambulance-chasing companies[60] were told not to chase ambulances anymore and then the loan consolidation companies were restricted from consolidating. Colin tried a more stock-specific approach, but the small caps he purchased often announced within days that they were 'in talks with bankers pending financial clarification'.

But Colin wasn't finished yet. As his worst falling knives were small caps, he fine-tuned his strategy. He would now focus on large caps. His timing was perfect and he didn't have to wait long for his first opportunity. The credit crisis knocked the shares of many banks to very low levels and Colin bought them. After all, his books explained that diversifying amongst cheap banks was always a successful strategy. However, Colin came unstuck as market capitalisation/operating profits, dividend yield, and finally price/net asset value all failed him as reliable indicators of value. Colin was mortified.

---

[60] Those companies that assist accident victims in claiming (typically dubiously high levels of) damages.

"Patience was the key. Wait until the stocks represent option value and then swoop"

Colin felt he had one more roll of the dice. The pressure was on and he really needed to deliver the goods. He decided now was not the time to be taking excessive risk. Instead, he would change strategy (or 'evolve' as he told his boss) and buy only grinding underperformers from the large cap universe. He'd had enough of volatility. In future he would eschew excitement and settle for 'get rich slow'. No more falling knives for him, 'bruised franchises'[61] were his game. He immediately went overweight large pharmaceutical and oil companies.

Sadly, Colin didn't survive to see the results of his new strategy. He was purged in the cuts of summer 2011 when the food price inflation crisis hit the markets hard. Ironically, Colin's recent performance was pretty good. Unfortunately for him, though, his client base was now tiny and his company needed his fund to seed a new investment opportunity in a global timber fund.

Happily though, Colin discovered, as an ex-fund manager, he was in much demand as a non-executive in the investment companies market. Colin returned to his native Guernsey and before you could say 'free lunch' was on the boards of 17 investment companies. Colin had never been happier or richer and was soon learning quickly about a wide range of 'alternative assets'. Admittedly, few of them performed any better than equities, but as an ex-fund manager Colin appreciated how important luck was in the investment process.

One day a few years later Colin opened his *FT* app to study some share prices. He was eager to see how much money his get rich slow strategy would have made for his investors *if only…*

---

[61] A phrase I use to describe companies with good brands, but which have badly lost their way through mismanagement.

No, he shouldn't go there. He wasn't bitter, so why care? But he was intrigued, so he looked at a few share prices.

He couldn't believe his eyes. He assumed there must have been some share consolidations to explain some of the share prices. But no, he double-checked the market caps. They really were **down** as much as he had originally thought. What on earth had happened?

It had not been a comfortable few years for mega caps. Despite their long-term underperformance and their strong value characteristics, conditions had gone from bad to worse. His favoured pharmaceutical companies had been promoting a number of their drugs for 'off-label' use. The industry had been warned (and fined) for this several times but had always paid their fines and moved on. This time, however, the politicians and the regulators had really thrown the book at them. When it then surfaced that a number of companies had manipulated their clinical data over many decades to purposely mislead about the efficacy of their drugs (many of which proved to be no more beneficial than the alternatives but a great deal riskier) the powers that be decided enough was enough. Fines of over US$300bn were finally agreed – not enough to bankrupt the companies, but sufficient to virtually destroy the value for equity holders.

The oil companies had suffered a similar tale of woe. A culture of indiscipline in health and safety had developed over many years, resulting in some terrible oil spillages. Politicians had experienced this before and had realised too late that the fines they imposed, whilst seemingly large, were a mere *bagatelle* for the companies given their size. This time they did not hold back and the industry received record fines. However, the bad news did not end there. The upstanding governments in many of the regions in which the companies operated did not wish to be associated with such poor corporate governance, and within the space of two years the industry found that its operations in Nigeria, Kazakhstan, Libya, Gabon,

Venezuela, Tunisia, Uganda, and Algeria had been confiscated. They were now mid cap exploration companies with stretched balance sheets.

Colin leant back in his seat. Wow! Was nothing safe? Was there tail risk in everything? He was a lot happier in the low risk world of non-exec positions. Now, where was he? Oh yes, there was a fascinating presentation he had been sent by a hedge fund that one of his companies invested in. It was highlighting the various methods to enhance portfolio performance using derivatives. If only everything were this straightforward, he thought.

December 2010

The 12 myths of investment – a presentation[62]

Today, I will highlight some areas of investment advice that I believe are accepted as standard investment dogma. Typically, these words of advice sound sensible and intuitively appealing. They may do – but I also believe they are **completely incorrect**.

So let's look at 12 of these myths.

Myth 1 – *'One must be intelligent to thrive in the investment jungle.'* You often hear fund managers lauded for their intelligence. However, virtually everyone in the City has a certain (high) level of intelligence. Surely intelligence only counts if one can take advantage of dumb people. If there **are** dumb investors around, I certainly haven't bumped into them.

I think intelligence is overrated. After all, look at the current financial crisis. Clever people created many of the toxic assets that have brought the financial world to its knees. And their cleverness is accompanied by dollops of overconfidence that convinced them that everyone else was wrong. As is usual, Warren Buffett hit the nail on its head: "If you have a 150 I.Q., sell 30 points to someone else. You need to be smart, but not a genius."

Myth 2 – *Ask the average investor what sort of companies they like to invest in and the answer is fairly standard: 'Invest in good companies with strong market positions, good management, a competitive advantage, excellent cash flow and strong balance sheets.'*

---

[62] I have given this presentation a number of times since 2008 – most recently to the 'Skeptics in the Pub' at The Maypole in Cambridge.

Quite clearly this is a sensible aspiration. However, it is a common aspiration and therefore a very crowded space. With everyone desperately searching for this sort of investment, there is no chance of it coming cheap and as it often comes expensive, it becomes a much higher risk purchase. Yet, this does not deter investors in the slightest and therefore provides us with a great opportunity ... and that is to do the opposite.

That opposite is to invest in companies currently regarded as poor, but which could become good. The great thing about these investments is they tend to be much cheaper than the first group.

Myth 3 − *'Avoid investing in companies you don't understand.'*
While this sounds obvious, it is rather harder to set the rules. After all, we are never in a position to be 100% knowledgeable about a subject, but obviously as soon as we are less than 100% we are in a position where we don't know how much we don't understand!

So where do we draw the line?[63] Perhaps investors often decide what they wish to invest in **and then** convince themselves they understand it. Bernie Madoff and his hedge fund is a good example here. Investors sought consistent positive returns and wanted to believe they were achieved at a low level of risk − they therefore convinced themselves that they understood Madoff's strategy.

To overcome these problems, we believe it is essential to appreciate one's levels of ignorance may be dangerously high. One way of dealing with that is to ensure that many different scenarios are considered prior to making an investment.

---

[63] For example, we know that Sainsbury's makes money from sales of jam tarts, bananas, and tinned tuna, but we do not know the precise mix. In these cases, we must form a view on how important the information we do not know could be to the final outcome. There is no doubt that what we don't know about a bank can hurt us much more than what we don't know about a food retailer.

Myth 4 – '*It is very important to meet management before making an investment.*'

The implicit assumption here is that management will tell us some company secrets (which is illegal) or that we can successfully judge their management skills. Instead, we run the risk of falling for their charm (especially if they laugh at all our jokes) or falling for their lies.

It is essential not to overestimate one's ability to analyse other people. More useful information can be gleaned by studying the numbers (for example, a balance sheet or a cash flow statement), rather than listening to the words and spin that accompany these numbers. And always remember that luck may have contributed significantly to an individual's success.

Myth 5 – '*A view on the economic outlook is essential if one is building a portfolio.*'

This straightforward assertion misses a few basic points. First, economic forecasting is extraordinarily difficult. There really is no evidence the major economic variables can be correctly forecasted consistently. However, even if it was possible, that is not good enough in terms of building a portfolio. One then has to select those stocks that are most likely to benefit from that outlook. And if the economic outlook is proved to be wrong a manager runs the risk of having all his stocks in the portfolio for the wrong reason. We adhere to the beliefs of Peter Lynch of Fidelity Magellan fame, who said anyone spending 15 minutes a year on macroeconomics has just wasted 12 of them. And famous economist J.K. Galbraith espoused similar views:

> "The only function of economic forecasting is to make astrology look respectable."

Instead, we believe selecting a number of cheap stocks across a number of industries and purchased at different times for different reasons is a lower risk approach.

Myth 6 – '*Shares should only be purchased with a catalyst.*'
This is a very popular belief which, as I understand it, is useful to avoid falling into what are commonly known as 'value traps' (a condition where a share keeps falling despite appearing cheap). Unfortunately, in over 20 years of searching, I have been unable to find a foolproof list of catalysts. Sure, they all seem to be highlighted in fund manager end of year reports, but this entails the use of hindsight. Clearly this is not a tool that is available at the time of investment. And let's face it, if everyone has correctly highlighted a sure-fire catalyst then the shares will have reacted instantaneously to its occurrence.
I've got no great intellectual comeback to this love of catalysts – all I can say is 'catalystshmatalyst'. Instead of desperately searching for these catalysts, we believe time can be more valuably spent looking for shares that are trading at a significant discount to fair value, even if it is not obvious what is going to move them. Let the market decide that.

Myth 7 – '*When share prices are going up, the "trend is your friend".*'
All that is apparently needed is a ruler and a pencil and one can draw a line that informs the analyst when to hold and when to sell. This might work if the position of the line was obvious, but from my experience, give ten chartists a ruler and they will draw at least 20 different trend lines. I know some people swear by charts ... and good luck to them.
We believe that charts are best left to the astrologers.

Myth 8 – '*When a share price is falling, always operate with a stop loss.*'
So, for example, if you purchase a share for £1 and the share price falls to 90p you should immediately sell and therefore limit your potential loss. This sounds very sensible and appears to ensure that no significant losers impact a fund's performance.

However, is it really right to be that mechanistic? Having bought a share for a good reason at £1 why on earth sell it just because it falls to 90p? After all, that is simply reflecting the fact that another investor is selling at a lower price. But there is no reason to believe that someone knows more than you do. It is very possible that we have made a mistake – so a share price fall alerts us to that risk and encourages us to rework our analysis. But following that, we may actually believe we are getting an even more attractive investment opportunity.

Myth 9 – *'Don't catch falling knives.'*
This suggests that falling share prices only ever fall further and clearly we know this is ridiculous. So why do people say it? I think it is because our worst mistakes emotionally scar us. Everyone has a war story about how they lost all their money after having a punt in a bombed out tech stock, or a bank, or even a biotech stock that then continued to fall precipitously. However, they are not looking at the whole universe of falling shares – simply remembering their worst ever experience. I also wonder if those people who suggest it is wrong to catch falling knives do not participate in Christmas sales or bid below the asking price for a house.
There is no alternative other than to analyse individually each falling knife and assess its merits. Sometimes we will buy more. At other times we won't. But it is incredibly simplistic to say *never* **do it.**

Myth 10 – *'Sell your losers and run with your winners.'*
Well, this implies valuations are irrelevant and that studying share prices alone is sufficient.
This misses the point that the market isn't always correct. Today's winners are often tomorrow's losers and today's losers are often tomorrow's winners. Both losers and winners are welcome on the portfolio providing they are cheap.

Myth 11 – '*Sell on the first profits warning or a dividend cut because it is bound to be followed by further bad news.*'

This 'rule' has become so well known that the amount of selling on the first warning is so great as to often discount a second and third profits warning. Perhaps this is an example of a strategy that worked well once, but now that it is in common use, no longer works.

We believe it is more profitable to study the positives when most are studying the negatives. Ask yourself whether it could be those positives that soon start to drive the share price forward.

Myth 12 – '*Trust your instinct.*'

To me, talking about feelings in the stock market is no different from having a feeling that you are going to win the lottery or that the dog in trap four is going to win. To us, this appears ludicrous. It's a bit like saying I can't be bothered to do any work so I'll just guess.

We believe feelings are for therapists.

In summary, I would say that rules don't work. If they did, then taken to the extreme, it would make investing very easy as analysis would be no longer be necessary – we'd all just type the relevant parameters into our computers and sit back. However, we think if investors concede to fixed rules and computing technology that must surely make it just a little easier for the rest of us.

But that is not to say these 12 'rules' are not commonly used. I believe they are, and moreover that many investors use them. This suggests running with the herd is a very dangerous strategy. Exactly how dangerous this is can be ascertained from the statistic that the majority of funds underperform the index over the long run.

It is therefore essential to do something different from the herd. We focus on out-of-favour stocks that other investors believe will fall even further out of favour, yet we believe are significantly under-valued. We call this approach contrarian investing.

Original thinking

Q. There is a lot of pressure within investment management to follow the herd – how have you avoided that? From being at a supportive company? Or building up a long track record with investors? A certain mental toughness? Or something else altogether?

Alastair: I think you need to be fundamentally comfortable with your investment process so that at times of greatest stress (when impostors are uncovered) you can continue to think rationally and objectively. Of course this necessitates enduring periods of underperformance and it also requires your employers and clients to similarly endure it. I think if you have articulated your investment process both those parties will (hopefully) provide you with sufficient time to show that you are not insane.

Q. Have you ever been tempted to tweak this process? For example, when the market appears to be valuing other metrics?

Alastair: Yes, we are always tweaking away, although we aim to tweak more when we are doing well as the tweaks are likely to be better quality if implemented when times are not too stressful. Making process changes when under pressure is often more a sign of appeasing unhappy groups. At those times inactivity is probably the better choice. We position ourselves as committed to our philosophy but with an evolutionary process and a flexible attitude to the stocks we hold.

Q. When you were building your process, how did you determine that it would work? Trial and error? Back-testing?[64]

Alastair: We looked back at history and asked how the most famous investors made money. Contrarian-based value investing came back loud and clear as one answer. But every value investor has their own style, even though they may adhere to the main principles of the style. We carried out extensive back-testing to

---

[64] Obviously our back-testing is of a much higher quality than those examples highlighted in the glossary.

understand the returns that might be generated from buying shares that have fallen very significantly and then combined these results with our valuation beliefs. This allowed us to take advantage of investors' behavioural biases as well as benefit from buying cheap stocks. And of course there was a lot of trial and error along the way. Learning from the mistakes we (and other people) have made has allowed us to concentrate on what we are better at and avoid what we are bad at. And this continues.

Q. Do you have a view on the most destructive clichés in investment management? (Things like 'I always meet management' or 'I only look at P/E ratios' etc., etc.)

Alastair: How long have you got?

1. 'It's cheap, but I can't see the catalyst'

2. 'There's a lot of uncertainty at the moment'

3. 'The future is unclear'

4. 'Always sell a stock on a profits warning'

5. 'A bull market climbs a wall of worry'

6. 'Diversification is a free lunch'

7. 'Buy equities for the long term'

8. 'It's time in the market, not timing the market that is important'

9. 'Don't catch falling knives'

10. 'The trend is your friend'

11. 'Don't fight the Fed'

12. '6000 (input number of choice) is an important psychological level'

13. 'Always have a stop loss'

14. 'Trust your instinct'

A Q&A for *Money Observer,* **February 2011**

Bye, bye Paddy

It is always difficult selling stocks such as Paddy Power; they have caused us no trouble in their time in the portfolio and are surrounded by a bullish glow as they leave. They were purchased when Irish stocks were very out of favour and at a time when investors were questioning how durable internet gambling would be in an economic downturn. But against this was a low valuation and a very strong balance sheet. In fact, the strong brand with its irreverent advertising – the 'Paddy Power can't get Tiddles back' advert attracted 1,089 complaints to the Advertising Standards Authority for the bizarre mix of both encouraging or condoning cruelty to animals and offensiveness to blind people – had a good recession and its internet business continued to grow strongly.

There are few negative outcomes for the future of Paddy Power that even our vivid imaginations can conjure up – an increasing tax rate for bookies or a catch up by other internet bookies, perhaps – but we must remain faithful to our valuation disciplines and sell at our estimate of fair value. We sell knowing we are passing it on to the momentum crowd, who will repeat all the well-known bull stories and claim they justify a much higher price, but like parents seeing their first-born daughter go away to university, we smile and move on.

January 2011

Can't give up the girl

The argument about Lloyds rests on whether retail banking is likely to produce great returns again. The bears have clearly voted on this, claiming increased balance sheet regulation will keep a lid on profitability. This may be accurate, but seems to be already discounted in the price. Banks have historically made good returns, in our view, because they have benefited from the financial illiteracy of their customers. Unless this illiteracy is eradicated or regulation is introduced to cap profitability, we believe the banks may be able to widen margins over the next few years, particularly given the diminution in competitive forces. While it is not a comfortable or riskless trade, at least the negatives are well aired in the market.

November 2009

Packing her in for good

Over the last few years, Lloyds in its various guises has been rather like an old girlfriend we cannot resist revisiting. The allure is the great retail banking franchise which, despite some enforced sell-offs, remains a highly profitable prize. This 'promised land' is offered to shareholders with a few caveats: a loan deposit ratio that needs to be reduced, a wholesale funding position over-reliant on short-term maturities and government guarantees, and a problem loan book that must be managed down.

Lloyds' management place all these problems in the 'nothing much to worry about' basket, but we are not so relaxed. Cut-throat competition for deposits seems set to continue, loan reduction through a reduction in good loans is a possible recipe for shrinking to failure, while a reduction in problem loans is much harder to stage manage. While credit investors are more willing to finance banks than a few years ago, there must be a risk that, as they are offered longer-term debt, they may demand their pound of flesh. The analyst community has swallowed the company line on these arguments, but we fear the risk of becoming a 'zombie bank' is very genuine for Lloyds and we have sold our position.

June 2010

It's just not cricket!

With markets going up, the sun out and the England cricket team successful, there seems to be considerably more positive spin being put on some fairly unchanged facts. (It should be borne in mind that the West Indies presence at Lord's is soon to be replaced by the mighty Australians. The stock market equivalent could prove equally scary.)

April 2009

Kissing frogs, and five other things

Everyone likes to avoid stress in their jobs and sleep well at night. In fund management, the difficulty of making decisions and the reaction these decisions generate in others affects one's state of mind. A decision that has proved hard to make because of an array of uncertainties and that contradicts the consensus can often be very uncomfortable and stressful. However, in the stock market this is not necessarily a bad thing. Typically, the easier the decision, the greater the chance that all of the positives are well known and fully discounted in the share price and, consequently, the comfort is borne from insufficient consideration of the negatives.

We believe it is vital to be comfortably uncomfortable with our decisions, *especially* if we know we are in a minority. Of course, that doesn't mean we should always fight the consensus, as often it is correct. The comfort must come from our rational analysis of the facts and compare well with the irrational pessimism of our competitors.

Investors are usually happier if they have acted after considering a large amount of relevant information. This intuitively seems more appealing than operating in an information vacuum. However, in most situations we drown in information – company reports and accounts, a plethora of broker reports on companies and meetings with management are just the tip of the iceberg. Internet stories, rumours, and speculation are plentiful. **Unfortunately, most of this information is simply noise, babble, and meaningless chatter and makes the decision-making process significantly more difficult.** Experience allows one to focus on the factors that are most likely to drive the share price in the future and ignore the transient information.

Any investment approach will have its good and bad times and, therefore, all fund managers are likely to provide their clients with both positive and negative experiences. (Sadly human nature being what it is, we seem to elicit most business from clients when we are doing particularly well; not an ideal starting point for those investors who dislike short-term disappointments.) Rather than pretending we are faultless world-beaters, **we prefer to spend time articulating our investment philosophy and process and, in particular, highlighting the conditions under which we struggle.** That way, clients will be better prepared for the bouts of underperformance that inevitably occur.

Humans are really good at some tasks and not so good at others. In many jobs that is just accepted. For example, consider a primary schoolteacher with incredible talents at teaching maths, but who struggles to educate his pupils in English. However, he must teach English – it is a mandatory part of the curriculum. This is very different to fund management, which permits one to opt out of areas that are too difficult. This is a fantastic luxury, but probably one that is not used enough. Fund managers are often confident people reluctant to admit to their areas of ignorance. They prefer instead to be seen as all-knowing Masters of the Universe. Fortunately, mistakes are acceptable in fund management (but best not to repeat them!) and, therefore, can teach us what we are good and bad at and shape our future behaviour. **Noting and learning from mistakes isn't a great experience and isn't a perfect way of building one's self-esteem, but it is a very worthwhile exercise if it reduces the chance of making mistakes.**

After making an investment, investors' brains seem to subconsciously commit to ignoring any new information that, however useful, contradicts their previous conclusion. **Instead, we try to remain ambivalent in our conclusion for as long as possible and in particular test the downside risk of any investment.** Sometimes you hear investors say, "There is no downside risk at all in these shares". This is usually a good signal that they either do not understand the company or are just blind to the risks.

As good as any investor may believe he is, the inconvenient truth is that he is in competition against a large number of people who have access to exactly the same information. Viewed in this way, one should be surprised to uncover many investment decisions in a

> "The inconvenient truth is that he is in competition against a large number of people who have access to exactly the same information"

normal year. It would be the equivalent of finding a £50 note lying on the pavement on Oxford Street on a busy Saturday afternoon. It is more logical to be moderately surprised when an interesting opportunity does arise. **Patience is, therefore, of absolute importance – it is essential to keep kissing lots of frogs – and typically there are no shortcuts to success.** The chance of finding a princess is fairly small, but if she does appear, we must make sure we cherish her.

September 2010

Postscript

As I re-read my commentaries written over the last four years, it strikes me that the compilation is the complete antithesis of an instruction manual. There are no lists, no must do's and don'ts and no acronyms to help navigate the reader through the investment jungle. Instead, I have simply shared some thoughts that have assisted me when trying to make sense of a welter of material. Investing is an art, not a science, and each investor takes their inspiration from a variety of diverse and, sometimes contradictory, sources. This inspiration doesn't always come at a desk; it can come at airport shops, whilst watching magicians, or even from chats with one's children.

There are many paths to the top of the mountain and it is vital that investors take the one best suited to their emotional make-up. For many investors, both amateur and professional, contrarian investing 'feels' right and therefore my thoughts will often chime with theirs. For others, I appear to be the devil incarnate. What look like tomatoes to me will just as clearly be tomaytoes in their eyes. And sometimes both parties, the believers and the naysayers, find it necessary to tell me just that…

The Audience Fights Back

From: Memact
Sent: Thu 18/08/2011 08:09
To: Alastair Mundy
Subject: Whimsy

I like these light-hearted pieces of whimsy: and the underlying implication that MUNDY STANDS ALONE unfazed by the vagaries of lemming-like market-makers, able to see through the short-term gloom and remaining focused on core values, which will come good (one day). (Surely one day you must be right, basic law of probability dictates that.)

✪ ★ ✪

From: Tony the Cabbie
Sent: 05 April 2011 06:26
To: Alastair Mundy
Subject: My Mother

I sent your commentary about me to my mother (the posh side of the family, my uncle Bob is her brother and ex-headmaster of a grammar school in Sussex). Her response is as follows…

—— Original Message ——

From: Tony's Mum
To: Tony the Cabbie
Sent: Monday, April 04, 2011 3:34 PM
Subject: Re: Fw: Monthly Report

Definitely sue. You are genetically programmed from both sides of the family to talk for England and be at least 96% accurate in your utterances. Your grandmother could talk the hind leg off a donkey, and on my side there's my uncle Frank who was good at chatting up 'old tarts', uncle Alec who covered worldwide political issues – not to mention your uncle Bob who can spout intelligent verbal diarrhoea until the cows come home.

❂ ★ ❂

From: John
Sent: 10 November 2011 10:24
To: Alastair Mundy
Subject: Carrots and hearing aids

Alastair,
I just want to say how much I enjoyed your piece in *Investment Week* about IPOs. I also loved the carrots versus light bulbs quote!
The piece has reminded me how messages can get lost or distorted along the way, and an item on the same that I used in my now defunct newsletter, *Investment Trust Scrutineer*:

> A lady was up before the Glasgow District Court charged with failing to keep a dog under control. Both she and the Clerk of the Court were slightly deaf, with the result that 'you have got a statutory warning' turned into 'your dog will be shot on Saturday morning' with predictably emotional results.

Regards, John

From: Annie in Marketing
Sent: Wed 09/11/2011 18:41
To: Alastair Mundy
Subject: Compliance

Hi Alastair

We tried – we really did, but the reference to 'transsexual' bars in Derby was flattened by marketing compliance. We have replaced it with Hells Angels![65]

Do hope this is ok for you. Shout if any issues as these will be uploaded to the web tomorrow.

From: Mum
Sent: 27 January 2011 08:38
To: Alastair Mundy
Subject: Chochem stuff

Dear Alastair,

Thanks for chochem piece. As usual I can't appreciate the content of your writing, but I know it's brilliant!

As with other Yiddish words, I think it's a shame the true meaning of the word's been lost – shnorrer's another!

Lots of love,

Mumxxxxxxxxx

---

[65] I have assumed the average reader is more open-minded than my compliance department and have therefore reverted to my original wording on page 59.

Further Reading – Build Your Own Book Mountain

Ariely, Dan, *The Upside of Irrationality: The Unexpected Benefits of Defying Logic at Work and at Home* (HarperCollins, 2010); and *Predictably Irrational: The Hidden Forces that Shape our Decisions* (HarperCollins, 2008)

How come everyone else is so dumb and irrational when we are so smart? Told at fast speed with moving auto-biographical inserts.

Burrough, Bryan, and John Helyar, *Barbarians at the Gate: The Fall of RJR Nabisco* (Arrow, 2004)

The story of the battle for RJR Nabisco. Impossible to make up.

Cialdini, Robert, *Influence: The Psychology of Persuasion* (HarperBusiness, 2007)

The classic on why people say yes. Written as a guide on how to spot sleazy sales techniques, but pounced upon instead by those wishing to employ them.

Damodaran, Aswath, *Investment Fables: Exposing the Myths of "Can't Miss" Investment Strategies* (Financial Times/Prentice Hall, 2004)

With the help of numerous academic studies Damodaran rather depressingly picks apart virtually every investment strategy ever voiced. It may be best to dip in and out of this one rather than commit yourself to a long innings.

Dreman, David, *Contrarian Investment Strategies* (Simon & Schuster, 1999)

All the proof you need to become a contrarian.

Einhorn, David, *Fooling Some of the People All of the Time: A Long Short Story* (John Wiley & Sons, 2008)

A hedge fund manager shorting a rotten company and the aggravation it entails.

Elkind Peter, and Bethany McLean, *The Smartest Guys in the Room: The Amazing Rise and Scandalous Fall of Enron* (Penguin, 2004)

The sorry tale of greed and yet more greed as a glamour stock turned into a falling knife.

Galbraith, John Kenneth, *The Great Crash 1929: The Classic Account of Financial Disaster* (Penguin, 2009)

An investment classic and easy reader.

Gawande, Atul, *Better: A Surgeon's Notes on Performance* (Profile Books, 2007); *Complications: A Surgeon's Notes on an Imperfect Science* (Picador, 2003); and *The Checklist Manifesto: How to Get Things Right* (Metropolitan Books, 2009)

Surgeon turned author takes us on a tour of the error-prone medical world and offers his solutions.

Gladwell, Malcolm, *Outliers: The Story of Success* (Penguin, 2009)

Covers some of the same ground as Syed's Bounce, but the message he delivers seems far more ambiguous. Then again, can over 4,000 positive reviews on Amazon really be wrong?

Jones, David, *NEXT to Me* (Nicholas Brealey Publishing, 2005)

The rags to riches story of the UK clothing retailer related by the Chief Executive of the recovery phase. Good for any contrarian investor who still believes buying at the bottom is easy.

Kahneman, Daniel, *Thinking, Fast and Slow* (Allen Lane, 2011)

The Godfather in the field of judgement and decision making reviews much of his academic work over many years and weaves in some interesting autobiographical stuff too.

Kasparov, Garry, *How Life Imitates Chess: Making the Right Moves, from the Board to the Boardroom* (Bloomsbury Publishing PLC, 2007)

The thinking man's Gazza explains the lessons he took from obliterating opponents on the chessboard to even tougher matches. He clearly loves a challenge – he's now a Russian politician.

Klarman, Seth A., *Margin of Safety: Risk-Averse Investing Strategies for the Thoughtful Investor* (HarperBusiness, 1991)

A legendary investor happy to tell everyone how he does it in the belief that, despite the evidence, few will change their behaviour.

Lewis, Michael, *The Big Short: Inside the Doomsday Machine* (W. W. Norton & Co., 2010)

Financial storyteller par excellence hunts down some winners from the Global Financial Crisis and en passant nails some losers. Twenty years after Liar's Poker he retains the ability to brilliantly explain complex concepts.

Lewis, Michael, *Liar's Poker: Rising Through the Wreckage on Wall Street* (W. W. Norton & Co., 1990)

An entertaining look at life on the inside of an investment bank. A must for every graduate trainee.

Lowenstein, Roger, *When Genius Failed: The Rise and Fall of Long-term Capital Management* (Random House Trade, 2001)

How a series of sensible-looking individual decisions led to a disastrous outcome that was entirely predictable.

Maier, Nicholas W., *Trading with the Enemy* (HarperCollins, 2002)

So, momentum investing can be successful – if you can handle the 4am starts and the nervous breakdowns!

Marks, Howard, *The Most Important Thing: Uncommon Sense for the Thoughtful Investor* (Columbia University Press, 2011)

Legendary fund manager brings together decades of his client memos to explain his secrets to successful investing. So simple you wonder why you bothered, until later when you realise how clever it is.

Matthews, Jeff, *Pilgrimage to Warren Buffett's Omaha: A Hedge Fund Manager's Dispatches from Inside the Berkshire Hathaway Annual Meeting* (McGraw-Hill Professional, 2008)

Not necessarily the best book on Buffett, but a highly readable description of the almost evangelical annual meeting of his company. Almost makes you want to purchase a highly over-priced plane ticket and hotel room and attend yourself.

Mauboussin, Michael J., *Think Twice: Harnessing the Power of Counterintuition* (Harvard Business School, 2009); and *More Than You Know: Finding Financial Wisdom in Unconventional Places* (Columbia University Press, 2006)

Legg Mason strategist blends findings from all walks of life to produce some fascinating thoughts on how to become a better investor.

Menschel, Robert, *Markets, Mobs and Mayhem: A Modern Look at the Madness of Crowds* (John Wiley & Sons, 2002)

A plethora of essays perfect for those with Attention Deficit Disorder covering mad behaviour in financial markets, and, even more worryingly, society.

Myers, David, *Intuition: Its Powers and Perils* (Yale University Press, 2002)

Does intuition work? By the end even the author seems confused, but plenty of material to start a good argument.

Neff, John, *John Neff on Investing* (Wiley, 1999)

Thirty-one years at the helm of the largest mutual fund in the US. Extraordinary how a book of 288 pages can be boiled down to 'buy low P/E stocks'.

Paulos, John Allen, *A Mathematician Plays the Market* (Allen Lane, 2003)

A thoroughly entertaining read recounting the huge losses made in WorldCom by a seemingly intelligent rational investor.

Ratner, Gerald, *The Rise and Fall...and Rise Again* (Capstone, 2007)

The riches to rags story of the UK jewellery company. For anyone eager to find where hubris takes you.

Richard, Christine S., *Confidence Game: How A Hedge Fund Manager Called Wall Street's Bluff* (John Wiley & Sons, 2010)

A hedge fund manager, Bill Ackman, sells (shorts) shares in a financial company convinced it is rotten to the core, and the roller-coaster journey to proving he is right.

Ronson, Jon, *The Psychopath Test: A Journey through the Madness Industry* (Picador, 2011)

Funny, worrying, thought-provoking ... and guaranteed to leave readers wondering about the psychopaths in their lives.

Rubin, Robert, and Jacob Weisberg, *In an Uncertain World: Tough Choices from Wall Street to Washington* (Random House Trade, 2004)

A Buffett recommendation and well worth it – a lucid explanation on how weighing the odds rather than solid conviction governs decision making.

Russo, J. Edward and Paul J.H. Schoemaker (1992), 'Managing Overconfidence', *Sloan Management Review*, pp 33, 7-17

A couple of academics concisely offer some ways of protecting us from the human curse of overconfidence.

Schulz, Kathryn, *Being Wrong: Adventures in the Margin of Error* (Ecco Press, 2010)

How can we be so wrong about so much and believe we are so often right?

Stewart, James Brewer, *Den of Thieves* (Simon & Schuster, 1992)

Milken, Boesky, high yield, insider dealing ... who needs novels when real life throws up these characters?

Syed, Matthew, *Bounce: The Myth of Talent and the Power of Practice* (Fourth Estate, 2011)

Table-tennis superstar unravels the make-up of a champion – nature or nurture?

Taleb, Nassim Nicholas, *Fooled by Randomness: The Hidden Role of Chance in Life and in the Markets* (Penguin, 2007)

A great book by an author not lacking in self-confidence. I think it would probably have been an even better read if he had allowed his publishers a chance to edit his work properly, but the book still conveys the importance of luck.

Willetts, David, *The Pinch: How the Baby Boomers Took Their Children's Future – And How They Can Give it Back* (Atlantic Books, 2010)

A fascinating read explaining how the baby boomers have benefited at the expense of the following generation. The reader is left wondering if Conservative Central Office deleted the chapters explaining the actions necessary to correct the issues the MP raises.

And finally:

Munger, Charles T., *Poor Charlie's Almanack: The Wit and Wisdom of Charles T. Munger* (Donning Company Publishers, 2005)

Not a man unaware of his abilities, but jewels scattered generously throughout this very large book. And if all else fails, it is a superb platform from which to start a serious book mountain.

Glossary

Anomaly switch

Originally used in the UK government bond market (gilt market) to describe the sale of one gilt and the simultaneous purchase of another. Theoretically the prices of the two gilts have a fairly stable long-term relationship, which can temporarily break down and provide an opportunity for an anomaly switch. An unsuccessful anomaly switch often evolves into a long-term investment!

Arbitrage

A term that, in its purest sense, describes an opportunity to generate profits by selling an asset in one market and simultaneously purchasing the same asset in another market. The profit is crystallised when the difference between the prices of the two assets narrows and the buy and sell are reversed. With the advent of electronic information this no longer occurs and an arbitrage now represents, to most practitioners, a bet on a relationship between two similar assets returning to a historical average (see also 'anomaly switch').

Attribution

This provides an investor with the information needed to assess how each stock (or sector, region, etc) within a portfolio has contributed to, or detracted from, performance. Fund managers are sometimes asked to provide clients with various breakdowns of this data, although it is unclear how they use it.

Back-testing

An exercise to find (what are usually) spurious mathematical relationships between asset classes. Having discovered a successful back-test, an investment bank will typically ditch other less successful back-tests and promote their favourite to the asset management industry. History informs us that the relationship typically breaks down not long after the end of the promotion period.

Barriers to entry

Describes certain properties of a business that comprise obstacles to prospective competitors. Barriers to entry may include, for example, brand names, patents, or the geographic location of the business. Sometimes governments introduce regulation to reduce barriers to entry and promote competition.

Dogs

Bad investments. It is usually necessary to blame the purchase of a dog on someone else.

Economies of scale

The benefits of size. These can be generated by, for example, purchasing supplies more cheaply than smaller competitors. Economies of scale often look most attractive on paper – in real life they are often mitigated by the negative consequences of becoming larger, such as increased levels of bureaucracy.

Enterprise value (EV)/sales

The value of a company's shares, debt, pension deficit and other nasties divided by the sales of the company. To the extreme value investor, the lower the ratio, the greater the potential for exciting profits from purchasing the shares. It is, however, worth bearing in mind that a company often looks cheapest in EV/sales terms just before it goes bust.

Ex-ante

What is expected to occur. Not as useful as ex-post – what actually happened.

Fair value

An individual's assessment of a company's worth (in contrast to current value, which informs an investor what the market believes the company is worth). Professional investors typically discuss fair value in a way that suggests it is a precise calculation. In reality, it is an educated guess.

Falling knife

A term usually used pejoratively to describe a share falling precipitously. 'Don't catch a falling knife' is one of the stock market's best known aphorisms, but is worryingly naïve in our opinion!

Gearing

A company takes on debt to develop its gearing. In some market conditions gearing is considered very positive and an opportunity to grow company profitability faster than otherwise possible. At other times it is viewed as the devil incarnate.

Holding period

The length of time that a share is held in a portfolio. Lower dealing costs and increased news flow have reduced holding periods significantly over the last thirty years.

Index hugging

The art of creating a portfolio that looks strangely similar to the stock market index against which the fund manager is measured. This is another pejorative term that suggests the fund manager is securing an exorbitant fee despite taking little risk.

IPO (initial public offering)

A modern term – we used to call them 'new issues' when the government was busy privatising industries – describing the sale (or partial sale) of a company to new shareholders with the shares subsequently listed on the stock market. My general rule of thumb is don't bother.

Like-for-like sales (LFL)

A way of measuring a company's operational performance over two similar time periods, but which focuses only on those assets (such as shops) that the company has been running over both periods. While great attention is paid to this statistic it can be easily manipulated. It may therefore be wiser to be concerned by a negative LFL than be impressed by a positive LFL.

Loss leader
A product priced very cheaply to entice customers. The customer is then susceptible to purchasing higher priced products. This a trick that supermarkets have used for years, although recent evidence suggests customer scepticism is growing.

Mega caps
A very large company (as measured by the value of its shares). No precise definition exists – it depends simply on what the user of the term is trying to prove.

Multi-bagger
A share that increases by a multiple of its starting value; for example, rising from 10p to 50p. While I have had a few in my career, I have spent a great deal of time bemoaning the many that I missed.

Negative surprise
A disappointment. The City seems incapable of using negative words in isolation and often adds a more positive word to provide a veneer of acceptability.

Pricing power
The term is typically used positively to highlight those companies that are able to push their prices higher without the fear of falling volumes offsetting the price increases. Often these companies have high barriers to entry.

Return on capital
The amount of profit generated by a company divided by the amount of money the company has invested to generate the profits.

Share split
Sometimes a company's board of directors believe their company's share price is too high. They 'correct' this by splitting each share into a greater number of shares, thus reducing the value of each new share. The financial position of investors is unaffected as they simply now own more shares at a lower price. It is very possible that there are more useful things for boards of directors to do.

Short; shorting

The hair-raising strategy of selling something you don't own (with the intention of buying it back at a lower price at a later date) and therefore laying yourself open to the prospect of unlimited losses. I would not recommend shorting individual shares unless the reader has masochistic tendencies or enjoys not sleeping.

Spin-off

The separation of part of a company into a company in its own right. This can be implemented by either an IPO or by giving shares in the spin-off to shareholders in the mother company.

Star fund manager (SFM)

A fund manager possessing apparently mystical abilities to significantly outperform his/her competition. Wait long enough and those abilities have a nasty habit of waning.

Stock lending

The action of lending shares to another investor to allow them to short the shares. The lender receives a fee and can call the stock back at any time. Non-believers find it odd that an investor would wish to lend his stock to someone whom he knows wishes to force the share price down.

Stop-loss

Used quite widely by amateur investors to limit losses. An investor sets a price, modestly below his purchase price, at which he will automatically sell the shares.

Tail risk

Very significant events which have only a small probability of crystallising. Underperforming investors usually highlight this in an apparent effort to categorise their occurrence as 'jolly bad luck'.

Value investing

A method of investing popularised by luminaries including Ben Graham and the young Warren Buffett that uses simple metrics such as dividend yield or price earnings ratios to derive the value of a company. Diametrically opposed, many would claim, to growth investing, which seeks to identify those companies with the greatest growth prospects.

Value trap
A share that continues to fall further despite looking cheap, thus encouraging further investment. Sometimes a supposed value trap morphs into a multi-bagger.